FACE THE ISSUES

Second Edition
Intermediate Listening
and Critical Thinking Skills

Carol Numrich

in cooperation with National Public Radio

 LONGMAN

Face the Issues: Intermediate Listening and Critical Thinking Skills, Second Edition

Longman, 10 Bank Street, White Plains, NY 10606-1951

NPR and Longman have tried unsuccessfully to locate the copyright owners of the introductory background music used on the cassette for Unit 5. It is therefore included without permission or credit. Longman accepts responsibility and welcomes any information as to its source.

The profiles in Unit 5 were adapted from *New York* magazine, December 21, 1981.

Acknowledgments can be found on page 187.

Editorial Director: Joanne Dresner
Senior Acquisitions Editor: Allen Ascher
Development Editor: Penny Laporte
Production Editor: Karen Philippidis
Text design: Curt Belshe, Naomi Ganor
Cover design: Naomi Ganor
Text art: Lloyd P. Birmingham, Robin Hessel Hoffmann, Donna Johnson
Photo research: Elizabeth Barker, Polli Heyden, Karen Philippidis

We wish to thank the following for providing us with photographs or artwork: Page 1, Pike Place Market/Preservation and Development Authority; Page 15, National Center for Health Statistics; Pages 27 and 32, Robert Armstrong; Page 38, © M. Burgess; Page 51, Deborah Robinson, 1989; Page 81, © Ron Romanosky/Greenpeace; Page 93, Photo courtesy of the Museum of the Hudson Highlands (Cornwall, NY). Indian garments by Nancy Red Star. Photograph by Joseph H. Kiley; Page 106, National Education Association; Page 123, David Brownell, © State of New Hampshire 1986; Page 135, Tim and Adam Gaes, from *My book for kids with cansur,* copyright 1987 by Jason Gaes, reproduced by permission, Melius & Peterson Publishing, Inc. (For more information, call 800-882-5171.); Pages 150, U.S. Army

Library of Congress Cataloging-in-Publication Data
Numrich, Carol.
    Face the Issues : intermediate listening and critical thinking skills / Carol Numrich, in cooperation with National Public Radio.—2nd ed.
        p. cm.
    ISBN 0-201-84672-1
    1. English language—Textbooks for foreign speakers.   2. Critical thinking—Problems, exercises, etc.   4. Listening—Problems, exercises, etc.   5. Readers—Current events.
I. National Public Radio (U.S.)   II. Title.
PE1128.N84   1996
428.3'4—dc20   96-28064
                                                                                                                   CIP

4 5 6 7 8 9 10 CRS 01 00 99 98

CONTENTS

INTRODUCTION

Face the Issues: Intermediate Listening and Critical Thinking Skills consists of twelve authentic radio interviews and reports from National Public Radio. The broadcasts were taken from *All Things Considered* and *Morning Edition*.

Designed for intermediate students of English as a Second Language, the text presents an integrated approach to developing listening comprehension and critical thinking skills. By using material produced for the native speaker, the listening selections provide content that is interesting, relevant, and educational. At the same time, they expose the nonnative speaker to unedited language, including the hesitations, redundancies, and various dialectical patterns that occur in everyday speech.

Each unit presents either a dialogue or a discussion of an issue of international appeal. The students gain an understanding of American values and culture as they develop their listening skills. Throughout each unit, students are encouraged to use the language and concepts presented in the listening material and to reevaluate their point of view.

SUGGESTIONS FOR USE

The exercises are designed to stimulate an interest in the material by drawing on students' previous knowledge and opinions and by aiding comprehension through vocabulary and guided listening exercises. In a variety of discussion activities, the students finally integrate new information with previously held opinions.

1 Predicting

In this exercise, students are asked to read the title of the interview or report and predict the content of the unit. This exercise should take a very short time—two or three minutes.

Some of the titles require an understanding of vocabulary or idiomatic expressions that the teacher may want to explain to the students. The ideas generated by the students can be written on the chalkboard. Once the students have listened to the interview or report, they can verify their predictions.

2 Think Ahead

Before listening to the tape, students are asked to discuss the issues to be presented in the interview or report. In groups of four or five, the students discuss their answers to general questions or react to statements that include ideas from the broadcast. The students draw on their own knowledge or experience for this activity. It is likely that students will have different opinions and that the discussion, especially with a verbal class, could become quite lengthy. It is recommended that the teacher limit this discussion to ten or fifteen minutes so as not to exhaust the subject prior to the listening activities.

3 Vocabulary

In this section, three types of exercises are presented to prepare the students for vocabulary and expressions used in the listening selection.

Vocabulary in a reading text. In these exercises, vocabulary is presented in a reading passage that also introduces some of the ideas from the broadcast. The students should read through the text once for global comprehension. Then, as they reread the text, they match the vocabulary items with synonyms or short definitions. The meaning of the new words may be derived from context clues, from general knowledge of the language, or from a dictionary.

Vocabulary in sentences. In these exercises, vocabulary is presented in sentences that relate to the ideas in the listening selection. Context clues are provided in each sentence. The students should first try to guess the meaning of these words by supplying their own definition or another word that they think has similar meaning. Although the students may not be sure of the exact meaning, they should be encouraged to guess. Once they have tried to determine the meaning of these words through context, they match the words with definitions or synonyms.

Vocabulary in word groups. These exercises focus on the relationship between specific vocabulary items from the listening selection and other words. A set of three words follows a given vocabulary item; in each set, two words have similar meaning to the vocabulary item. It is suggested that the students work together to discuss what they know about these words. Through these discussions, they will begin to recognize roots and prefixes and how these words relate to each other. The students should be encouraged to use a dictionary for this exercise.

4   Task Listening

This exercise presents the students with a global comprehension task before asking them to focus on more specific information in the listening selection. The "task" is purposely simple to help students focus on an important point in the recorded material. Consequently, most of the students should be able to answer the questions after the first listening.

5   Listening for Main Ideas

The second time students hear the recorded material, they are given questions to guide them in comprehending the main ideas of the listening selection. Each interview or report has between three and six main ideas that have been used to divide the selection into Parts. Each Part is introduced by a beep on the tape. The students are asked to choose the answers that best express the main ideas. The teacher should stop the tape at the sound of the beep to make sure the students have chosen an answer. The students may then compare their answers to see whether they agree on the main ideas. Only one listening is usually required for this exercise; however, some classes may need to listen twice in order to agree on the main ideas.

6   Listening for Details

In the third listening, the students are asked to focus on detailed information. The students are first asked to read either true-and-false statements or multiple-choice questions. The teacher should clarify any items that the students do not understand. Then each Part of the recording is played. The students choose the correct answers as they listen, thus evaluating their comprehension. Then, in pairs, they compare answers. The teacher should encourage the students to defend their answers based on their comprehension. They should also be encouraged to convince the other students of the accuracy of their answers. There will certainly be disagreements over some of the answers; the discussions will help focus attention on the information needed to answer the questions correctly. By listening to each Part another time, the students generally recognize this information. Once again, they should be asked to agree on their answers. If there are still misunderstandings, the tape should be played a third time, with the teacher verifying the answers and pointing out where the information is heard on the tape. It is important to note that some of the questions require interpretation or inference.

7   Looking at Language

In this exercise, an interesting point of language from the recorded material is presented in isolation, as a further aid to comprehension. In each broadcast, the use of grammar, idioms, or another aspect of language is highlighted. The students are asked to listen to a segment from the listening selection and to focus on this use of language in context. Then, through discussions and exercises, the students practice the language in a different context. These exercises are not meant to be exhaustive, but rather to point out an interesting use of language. The teacher may want to supplement this exercise.

8   Follow-up Activities

In this section, three activities are presented. The teacher may want to choose only one or perhaps to choose one oral and one writing activity. The students should be encouraged to incorporate in their writing and discussions the vocabulary and concepts that were presented in the interview or report. It is expected that the students will synthesize the information gathered from the broadcast with their own opinions.

Discussion questions. In groups, the students discuss their answers to one or more of the questions. Students will most likely have different points of view, and it is during this discussion that they are given the opportunity to present their views to each other.

Essay topics. These topics give the students the opportunity to react in writing to the interview or report.

Interactive processing activities. Each activity begins with an optional listening and note-taking exercise in which the students listen to the interview or report again for important details. By listening with a particular focus, they will be better prepared to complete the final activities. These final activities consist of debates, case studies, role plays, values-clarification exercises, and other activities in which the students must solve problems or develop ideas that recycle the language and concepts in the interviews and reports. During these activities, the students will have an opportunity to examine creatively their beliefs about the issues presented.

If It Smells Like Fish, Forget It

1

1   PREDICTING

From the title, discuss what you think the interview is about.

2 | **THINK AHEAD**

In groups, discuss your answers to the following questions.

1. Do you eat fish? Do you ever buy or cook fresh fish?

2. Do you usually shop for fresh food? How do you decide whether certain foods are fresh? Give some examples.

3. What advertising techniques do supermarkets use to encourage you to buy food? How do they make food look fresher than it really is? Give some examples.

3 | **VOCABULARY**

Exercise 1

Look at the drawing of a fish. Read the vocabulary and definitions below. Then label each part of the fish on the drawing.

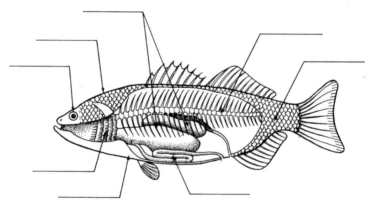

backbone: spine; line of bones down the middle of the back
belly: stomach; bulging part
eyes: organ of sight
scales: overlapping plates of hard material that cover the skin
viscera: internal organs of the body
slime: sticky substance on the surface of the fish
gill: organ with which a fish breathes
guts: intestines; bowels (verb: "to gut a fish")

Exercise 2

Read the following sentences. The highlighted words will help you understand the interview. Try to guess the meaning of these words from the context of the sentences. Then write a synonym or your own definition of the words.

1. Near the harbor, you can hear the ***fishmongers*** calling out the names of the fish they're trying to sell.

   _____

2. We could hear the beautiful-sounding ***chant*** coming from the cathedral on the hill.

   _____

3. He knows Italy very well, so he gave me some good ***tips*** on which towns to visit during my vacation.

   _____

4. She tasted the first dish her friend had ever cooked and said "Oh, this is ***yucky***. I don't think I can eat it!"

   _____

5. A fish must be ***slitted*** and cleaned out before you can cook it.

   _____

6. The waves in the ocean ***curl*** just before they break.

   _____

7. Most of his clothes were ***patchy*** because he had repaired them with so many different types of material.

   _____

8. If you leave food in the refrigerator too long, it will ***spoil***, and you won't be able to eat it.

   _____

(continued on next page)

9. When the archaeologists discovered the dinosaur bones, they were surprised that the whole skeleton had remained *intact*.

_____

10. He hadn't been in the sun all summer, so his skin was *pale*, unlike the other tanned tourists.

_____

Now try to match the words with a definition or synonym. Then compare your answers with those of another student. The first one has been done for you.

_j_	1. fishmongers	a.	cut open
____	2. chant	b.	a repeated tune; words repeated over and over
____	3. tips	c.	become bad
____	4. yucky	d.	undamaged; whole; complete
____	5. slitted	e.	unpleasant or disgusting
____	6. curl	f.	irregular; different from the surrounding parts; spotty
____	7. patchy	g.	little color; not bright
____	8. spoil	h.	twist; turn inward or roll up
____	9. intact	i.	suggestions
____	10. pale	j.	people who sell fish

4	**TASK LISTENING**

Listen to the interview. Find the answer to the following question.

> Which part of the fish (from the fish vocabulary on page 2) is, surprisingly, *not* a good indicator of how fresh a fish is?

5 | LISTENING FOR MAIN IDEAS

Listen to the interview again. The interview has been divided into five parts, each expressing a main idea. You will hear a beep at the end of each part. As you listen, circle the answer that best expresses the main idea in that part. Compare your answers with those of another student.

PART 1   What will we learn from this interview?

a. how to shop for fish

b. how to distinguish different types of fish

c. how to choose a fish man (supplier)

PART 2   How should a fish look when you buy it?

a. bloody

b. fat

c. flat

PART 3   How should a fish feel when you buy it?

a. slimy

b. icy

c. patchy

PART 4   Which part of the fish is a good indicator of freshness?

a. the eyes, when the fish has been on ice

b. the gills, when the fish is intact

c. the guts, when the fish has been slitted

PART 5   How should a quality fish market smell?

a. like a good fish environment

b. fishy

c. like nothing

LISTENING FOR DETAILS

*Read the statements for Part 1. Then listen to Part 1 again and decide whether the statements are true or false. As you listen, write a **T** or **F** next to each statement. Compare your answers with those of another student. If you disagree, listen again to Part 1.*

PART 1

_____ 1. Every red-blooded American knows how to buy fresh fish.

_____ 2. Even vegetarians should listen to this interview.

_____ 3. The interview takes place in Seattle.

_____ 4. Some customers come for the show more than the fish.

_____ 5. The fishmongers play football while they sell fish.

_____ 6. Brian Poor, a local chef, asks the fishmongers to inspect the fish for him.

Repeat the same procedure for Parts 2–5.

PART 2

_____ 7. Poor says the backbone area is the first place to look to see if a fish is fresh.

_____ 8. He doesn't want blood on the backbone.

_____ 9. Brown blood is a sign of an old fish.

_____ 10. No blood on a fish means it may have been washed.

_____ 11. A just slitted and cleaned fish has a flat belly.

_____ 12. An older fish's belly curls in on itself.

_____ 13. A fresh fish looks like it still has the viscera in it.

PART 3

_____ 14. The interviewer doesn't like slimy fish.

_____ 15. Melting ice will preserve slime on fish.

_____ 16. Slime is necessary for a fish's life.

_____ 17. The slimier the fish, the better.

_____ 18. The more scales there are on the fish, the less the fish has been handled.

PART 4

_____ 19. If a fish has been iced up, the eyes can be a good indicator of freshness.

_____ 20. You should never buy a cloudy-eyed fish.

_____ 21. A spoiled fish sometimes has glassy eyes.

_____ 22. The gills on a fish should be bloody.

_____ 23. Most gutted fish don't have gills intact.

_____ 24. The gills on a fish should be pale.

PART 5

_____ 25. Brian Poor sniffs a fish to judge its freshness.

_____ 26. If a fish market smells like fish, you should tell the fishmongers.

_____ 27. Fresh fish don't smell.

| 7 |

LOOKING AT LANGUAGE

■ COMPARATIVES

Exercise 1

Listen again to Mr. Poor's explanation of slime and scales on a fish. Focus on the structure in italics. Can you explain the meaning and usage?

ZWERDLING:
So, Brian Poor, the more slime the better.

POOR:
The more slime, the better.

ZWERDLING:
OK. What about scales? Sometimes people say—Any clue?

POOR:
The more they are handled, the more scales they lose.

EXPLANATION

In the example from the interview, Mr. Poor is using the comparative to show a cause-and-effect relationship. He is saying that:

1. If a fish has slime, it's a fresher (better) fish. So we want to shop for slimy fish.

2. If people handle fish, the fish lose their scales. So we want to shop for fish that still have their scales.

The structure for a ***cause-and-effect comparative*** is as follows:

THE	COMPARATIVE FORM	*THE*	COMPARATIVE FORM
The	more slime (there is),	the	better (it is).
The	more they are handled,	the	more scales they lose.
The	more a fish smells,	the	less fresh it is.

Exercise 2

Write sentences describing conditions for buying different foods. Use the structure described above and fill in the blanks.

1. It's not easy to shop for melons, but most people think that

   _____ the smell, _____ the melon.
       (sweet)   (delicious)

2. More and more people are concerned about the fat content in

   hamburger meat these days. Usually, _____ the color,
                   (red)

   _____ the meat.
      (lean)

3. I only buy peaches when they're in season. And _____
              (ripe)

   the peach, _____ it tastes.
        (good)

4. Not everyone agrees, but the French generally think that

   _____ the cheese, _____ its taste.
      (pungent)   (refined)

5. Red wine gets better over time. _____ you store it,
                     (long)

   _____ it tastes when you drink it.
      (smooth)

6. Good bread should be eaten the day it's bought. _____ you
                       (long)

   keep it, the _____ it will taste.
        (fresh)

Exercise 3

Read the sentences. Rewrite the information, using cause-and-effect comparative sentences. The first one has been done for you.

1. When a banana peel is still green, the banana is not yet ripe.

   The greener the peel, the less ripe the banana.

2. When a tomato looks very red, there's a chance it tastes rotten.

   _____

(continued on next page)

3. When produce is good quality, the cost is usually high.

_____

4. When fruit juice is natural, the taste is not so sweet.

_____

5. When raspberries look beautiful, they taste delicious.

_____

6. When food has additives, it lasts longer.

_____

7. When its interior is soft, an avocado is ripe.

_____

8   FOLLOW-UP ACTIVITIES

■ DISCUSSION QUESTIONS

In groups, discuss your answers to the following questions.

1. Do you care about the freshness of food? Will the information from this interview change the way you shop for fish or for any fresh food?

2. What tips would you give for buying fresh foods in your country?

■ ESSAY TOPICS

Choose one of the following topics.

1. How has the selling and buying of food changed over the years? Write an essay in which you describe these changes.

2. Write an essay in which you describe a product that you purchased and that you now regret purchasing. What do you know now that you should have known when you bought it? What advice would you give someone buying a similar product?

▧ TIPS FOR BUYING: HOW TO BUY A PRODUCT

A. Taking Notes to Prepare

By focusing on how to buy fresh fish, you may be better prepared to offer advice on buying other products in the follow-up exercise on page 13.

Listen to the interview again. Take notes on the important considerations in choosing fresh fish. Key phrases and some examples have been provided for you.

Who should inspect the fish:

the customer

_____

_____

_____

_____

Consideration of blood:

blood should be on the backbone

_____

_____

_____

_____

Consideration of the belly shape:

nice belly shape

_____

_____

_____

_____

(continued on next page)

Consideration of the outside of a fish:

the more slime, the better

_____

_____

_____

_____

Consideration of the eyes:

cloudy eyes not an indication of freshness

_____

_____

_____

_____

Consideration of the gills:

farm-raised fish come intact

_____

_____

_____

_____

Requirements of a quality fish supplier:

no smell when you sniff

_____

_____

_____

_____

B. Tips for Buying Things

In the interview, you heard about how to buy fresh fish. It's not always easy to know what to look for when buying a product you don't know well.

THE PRODUCT

Work in groups. Choose a product that you are familiar with. You may want to choose one of the products below, or you may choose one of your own.

Food

- chicken
- melons
- tomatoes
- grapefruits

Electronics

- computers
- VCRs
- stereos
- camcorders

Sports Equipment

- sneakers
- skis
- tennis rackets
- exercise machines

Home Appliances

- coffeemakers
- toasters
- washers/dryers

Vehicles

- used cars
- new cars
- motorcycles

Clothing

- designer versus imitation

(continued on next page)

THE PROCEDURE

Prepare a list of tips for buying the product. In preparing your list, consider the following:

- What should it look like on the outside?

- What should it be composed of on the inside?

- Which parts are of most interest?

- Which dealers/suppliers are the best?

- Who should give you advice on buying the product?

Present your tips to the class.

"If It Smells Like Fish, Forget It" was first broadcast on *All Things Considered*, November 19, 1994. The interviewer is Daniel Zwerdling.

LIVING THROUGH DIVORCE

2

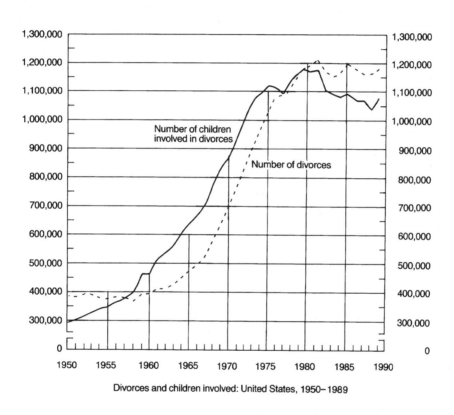

Divorces and children involved: United States, 1950–1989

Number of children involved in divorces

Number of divorces

---

1 | PREDICTING

From the title, discuss what you think the interview is about.

2 THINK AHEAD

In groups, discuss your answers to the following questions.

1. Look at the graph on page 15. How has the number of children involved in divorces in the United States changed since 1950?

2. Who suffers more in a divorce, parents or children?

3. Should parents who get divorced explain the reasons to their children?

3 VOCABULARY

Read the following sentences. The highlighted words will help you understand the interview. Try to guess the meaning of these words from the context of the sentences. Then write a synonym or your own definition of the words.

1. Children often feel alone and don't know who they can ***turn to*** when their parents get divorced.

   _____

2. It is difficult for children to ***get used to*** living with only one parent after their parents are divorced.

   _____

3. People often find it difficult to explain their reasons for divorce. Is it the parents' responsibility to ***share*** these reasons with their children?

   _____

4. When parents divorce they often have a difficult time ***reassuring*** their children and making them feel that everything will be all right.

   _____

5. A child's first dance or music ***recital*** is a big event. Children feel it is important for their parents to attend.

   _____

6. ***Guidance counselors*** work in schools to help children with their studies, but they sometimes help children with their family problems too.

   _____

7. Children suffer most when their parents first divorce; however, with time, they can usually **get through it**.

_____

8. Perhaps the most difficult time for children is the time when they see one of their parents **packing up** to leave the home forever.

_____

9. Children often think that their parents' divorce is their **fault**; they feel responsible for their parents' unhappiness.

_____

10. Authors sometimes decide to write a **series** of books if their first book has been successful.

_____

Now try to match the words and expressions with a definition or synonym. Then compare your answers with those of another student. The first one has been done for you.

___*b*___ 1. turn to

_____ 2. get used to

_____ 3. share

_____ 4. reassure

_____ 5. recital

_____ 6. guidance counselor

_____ 7. get through something

_____ 8. pack up

_____ 9. fault

_____ 10. series

a. performance

b. ask for help

c. responsibility for something bad

d. a person who gives advice to students

e. prepare to leave

f. survive something

g. tell others about your experiences

h. get into the habit of

i. comfort

j. a continuing group of books or events

| 4 | # TASK LISTENING |

Listen to the interview. Find the answer to the following question.

Why is Betsy concerned about divorce?

| 5 | # LISTENING FOR MAIN IDEAS |

Listen to the interview again. The interview has been divided into three parts, each expressing a main idea. You will hear a beep at the end of each part. As you listen, circle the answer that best expresses the main idea in that part. Compare your answers with those of another student.

PART 1   Why did Betsy Allison Walter write to the mayor about her parents' divorce?

a. She thought he was responsible for divorces in New York.

b. She thought he was a good parent and would understand.

c. She thought he knew a lot of things.

PART 2   How does Betsy feel about the advice that is given to her?

a. She realizes that she is the only child with her problem.

b. She still doesn't understand why her parents are getting divorced.

c. She now understands why her parents can't stay together.

PART 3   What advice does Betsy give other children in her book?

a. She tells them that it's their fault if their parents get divorced.

b. She tells them not to cry.

c. She says they should tell someone about their feelings.

6 | LISTENING FOR DETAILS

*Read the statements for Part 1. Then listen to Part 1 again and decide whether the statements are true or false. As you listen, write a **T** or **F** next to each statement. Compare your answers with those of another student. If you disagree, listen again to Part 1.*

PART 1

_____ 1. Betsy Allison Walter is nine years old.

_____ 2. Betsy lives in Manhattan.

_____ 3. Betsy had no one to turn to.

_____ 4. Betsy's father is with somebody else.

_____ 5. Mayor Koch wrote back to Betsy.

_____ 6. Mayor Koch gave her a solution to her problem.

_____ 7. His letter was reassuring to Betsy.

_____ 8. Betsy had hoped that the mayor would call her father.

_____ 9. Betsy's parents sat next to each other at her dance recital.

Repeat the same procedure for Parts 2 and 3.

PART 2

_____ 10. Four hundred kids in Betsy's school have the same problem.

_____ 11. The interviewer says most people have parents who are divorced.

_____ 12. *The Boys' and Girls' Book of Divorce* was written by a psychologist.

_____ 13. Betsy went out to buy his other book.

_____ 14. She loved his book.

_____ 15. Betsy feels satisfied with people's answers about divorce.

(continued on next page)

_____ 16. She thinks parents sometimes hide their reasons for divorce.

_____ 17. Her father left the house.

_____ 18. Betsy wants her parents to get divorced.

PART 3

_____ 19. Betsy wrote a short book of advice.

_____ 20. She reads the whole book in the interview.

_____ 21. The interviewer gives Betsy advice about her parents.

_____ 22. Betsy wants to be a writer and write a series of books.

_____ 23. She would like to be rich.

_____ 24. She would like to be famous.

7 LOOKING AT LANGUAGE

▪ LETTER WRITING

Exercise 1

There are seven basic parts to a letter. Read the following information about each part.

The date: In the United States, the date is written as: Month, Day, Year.

The sender's address: This is either printed on the top of the letter or typed on the top left side of the letter.

The salutation: This part opens the letter. It usually begins with "Dear. . . ."

The body: This is the main part of the letter. It includes one or more paragraphs.

Special greeting: This can finish your message. It comes at the end of the body of the letter.

The close: This is the expression we use to finish the letter, before signing our name.

The signature: If the letter is typed, this is always written by hand, in ink. In formal letters the name is typed below the signature.

Now listen to Mayor Koch's letter to Betsy. As you listen, focus on the different parts of the letter. Then work with another student and label each of the seven parts.

```
                          Office of the Mayor
                          The City of New York
                          New York, N. Y. 10007

February 11, 1987

Dear Betsy,

Thank you for the letter. I was
saddened to learn of the difficult
times you are experiencing now. It
is important for you to share your
feelings and thoughts with someone
during this time. I wish there was
an easy solution to these problems,
but there is not. Please remember
that you are loved and that people
care about you.

All the best.

Sincerely,



Edward Koch
```

Exercise 2

1. The following variations can occur within the different parts of a letter. The choice of expression depends on the formality of the letter.

Work as a class. Discuss these different expressions. Decide if the expression should be used in formal or informal letters. Then write it in the chart below. Try to think of other examples and add them to the chart.

Salutation:	Dear Eric,
	Dear Mr. McCarthy:
	Dear Sir:
	To whom it may concern:
Special greeting at the end:	All the best.
	I look forward to hearing from you.
	Take care.
	Write soon.
The close:	Love,
	Sincerely,
	Yours truly,
	Fondly,

Formal Expressions	*Informal Expressions*
Dear Mr. MCarthy:	*Dear Eric,*

2. Compare and contrast letter writing in your own countries to that in the United States. What expressions are used in opening and closing letters? In a letter, do you address people differently according to sex, profession, or relationship? How do you address different people in your country?

Exercise 3

Choose one of the following and write a letter.

1. Write your own letter to Betsy giving her advice on her problem.

2. Imagine that you heard this interview on the radio. Write a letter to the editor of your local newspaper. React to the advice given to Betsy about divorce.

8   FOLLOW-UP ACTIVITIES

▣ DISCUSSION QUESTIONS

In groups, discuss your answers to the following questions.

1. Betsy wanted her parents to sit together during her dance recital, but they didn't. In your opinion, do divorced parents have an obligation to be together at important times in their child's life?

2. In Betsy's school, 75 percent of the children have parents who are divorced (300 out of 400). This percentage is not unusual in the United States. How does this percentage differ from the divorce rate in your country? What are the reasons for the difference or similarity?

▣ ESSAY TOPICS

Choose one of the following topics.

1. Betsy's parents didn't explain to her their reasons for getting divorced. If you were Betsy's parents, would you discuss the reasons with her? Does it help children to accept their parents' divorce if they know the reasons for it? Write an essay in which you express your opinion.

(continued on next page)

2. Who is the best person to turn to when you experience pain: a friend, a parent, the school, the church? Write an essay in which you express your opinion and give your reasons.

■ CASE STUDIES: THE QUESTION OF DIVORCE

A. Taking Notes to Prepare

*Listen to the interview again. Take notes on the advice given to Betsy in the interview and her feelings about divorce. Key phrases and some examples have been provided for you. Use these notes to help you understand and prepare the issues in the **case studies** on pages 25–26.*

Advice given to Betsy:

It's important to share feelings.

_____

_____

_____

Persons giving advice to Betsy:

The mayor of New York

_____

_____

_____

Betsy's questions and feelings about divorce:

Who should she turn to?

_____

_____

_____

Betsy's advice to others:

It's not your fault.

_____

_____

_____

B. Case Studies

You have listened to a little girl express her feelings about her parents' divorce. You also have your own opinions on the issue of divorce.

Work in groups. Read each of the following cases. Then act as a group of family counselors. Discuss each case and agree on advice for each person. Take notes on your group's discussion. Then compare your suggestions with those of the other groups.

CASE 1: BETSY (AGE 8)

"My parents are getting divorced, and I really don't know who to turn to. My dad met another woman. I was just getting used to my life, and now this! It's really kind of hard on me. I invited both my parents to my dance recital, but they didn't sit next to each other. It was painful to see my dad packing up to leave. They won't explain anything to me."

CASE 2: GEORGE (AGE 66)

"My son has been married for ten years. His wife's a wonderful young woman. Over the years, my wife and I have grown quite attached to her. In fact, she's like a daughter to us. We've spent all the family holidays with them and we have even gone on vacations with them. Now, after ten years, my son has decided to go off with another woman. He is divorcing his wife so that he can be with this new woman. We are very fond of our daughter-in-law but don't know whether or not we should continue our relationship with her. Our son doesn't want us to continue seeing her."

(continued on next page)

CASE 3: CAROLYN (AGE 28)

"I married my husband five years ago. I was twenty-three years old . . . too young to know what I was doing. My life with him has become very boring. We never go out. We don't have any friends. I no longer want to be with him because we don't have anything in common. We have a two-year-old daughter, and I haven't wanted to think about getting a divorce. But I'm afraid that if my husband and I stay together, it will be even worse for her."

CASE 4: JOHN (AGE 44)

"I have been seeing a married woman for six months now. She's been in a very unhappy marriage for years and is going to be getting a divorce soon. We've fallen in love and want to spend as much time together as possible. The problem is that she has a son. Every time I go over to her house, I feel guilty because of her child. I know that he misses his father and doesn't appreciate me visiting his mother at the house. It's difficult for our relationship because we can't easily get together without her son. I don't know if I should continue this relationship until the divorce is final. In fact, I don't know if the relationship will ever work out because of her child and his relationship to his father."

CASE 5: JOYCE (AGE 50)

"I have been happily married for thirty years. This year my husband started acting differently toward me. He didn't seem to be interested in doing anything with me anymore. Finally I realized what had happened. He was seeing another woman. This other woman is half my age. She's twenty-five! I'm so depressed. I never thought that this could happen to me. My husband and I have discussed the matter; we've decided to get a divorce. My children are grown up and living on their own. I don't want to tell them about their father because I'm too ashamed."

"Living through Divorce" was first broadcast on *All Things Considered*, February 11, 1987. The interviewer is Noah Adams.

A Couch Potato

PREDICTING

From the title, discuss what you think the interview is about.

2   THINK AHEAD

In groups, discuss your answers to the following questions.

1. In your opinion, what is the best way to relax? Do you prefer watching TV, reading a book or magazine, or some other form of relaxation?

2. Do you spend time with your family during the holidays? What do you do together? Do you spend any of this time watching television as a family?

3. How much TV do you watch a week? Would you rather watch more or less? Why?

3   VOCABULARY

The following words will help you understand the interview. Try to guess the meaning of the words. Use your knowledge of English, or use your dictionaries. In each set of words, cross out the word that does not have a similar meaning to the highlighted word. Then compare your answers with those of another student. Discuss why these words are similar. The first one has been done for you.

1. **coin a phrase**	develop a name	create a term	~~print money~~
2. **junk food**	soda	potato chips	oatmeal
3. **head**	founder	secretary	president
4. **tolerate**	accept	endure	abandon
5. **hearth**	workplace	home	fireplace
6. **guilt**	wrongdoing	pride	shame
7. **tuber**	potato	underground root	disease
8. **icon**	ice	symbol	picture

9. **tube**	television	TV	telephone
10. **physique**	shape	build	chemistry
11. **ballast**	stability	weight	quality

4 | TASK LISTENING

Listen to the interview. Find the answer to the following question.

> What is an important time for couch potatoes?

5 | LISTENING FOR MAIN IDEAS

Listen to the interview again. The interview has been divided into four parts, each expressing a main idea. You will hear a beep at the end of each part. As you listen, circle the answer that best expresses the main idea in that part. Compare your answers with those of another student.

PART 1   What did Robert Armstrong do?

      a. He founded a club for people who like to watch TV.

      b. He started a club for cartoonists.

      c. He created a T-shirt company.

PART 2   Why are the holidays important for couch potatoes?

      a. Families go to football games together.

      b. Families turn off the TV.

      c. Families spend time together.

PART 3   Why is there a need for a club like the Couch Potatoes?

      a. People suffer from watching TV.

      b. People eat too many potatoes.

      c. People feel guilty about how much TV they watch.

(continued on next page)

PART 4   What kinds of TV program do couch potatoes watch?

a. only the most popular TV shows

b. programs on member stations

c. anything on TV

6   LISTENING FOR DETAILS

*Read the statements for Part 1. Then listen to Part 1 again and decide whether the statements are true or false. As you listen, write a **T** or **F** next to each statement. Compare your answers with those of another student. If you disagree, listen again to Part 1.*

PART 1

_____ 1. Robert Armstrong lives in California.

_____ 2. He coined the phrase "couch potato" in 1966.

_____ 3. The phrase seems old to the interviewer.

_____ 4. There are 8,500 couch potato clubs.

_____ 5. Members receive handbooks, newsletters, and T-shirts.

Repeat the same procedure for Parts 2–4.

PART 2

According to Robert Armstrong . . .

_____ 6. Men and women watch football games on TV during the holidays.

_____ 7. Families get along better if they watch TV.

_____ 8. Family members can never agree on a TV program to watch.

PART 3

_____ 9. Most people agree that watching TV is an intellectual activity.

_____ 10. Some people lie about how much TV they watch.

_____ 11. Robert Armstrong thinks couch potatoes should put their TVs in the closet.

_____ 12. The potato is the icon for couch potatoes.

_____ 13. Some couch potatoes get a potato shape from watching so much TV.

_____ 14. Robert Armstrong says couch potatoes roll off the couch easily.

PART 4

_____ 15. *Love Boat* is one of the favorite TV shows of couch potatoes.

_____ 16. Couch potatoes think that "if it's on TV, it must be good."

7 | LOOKING AT LANGUAGE

▒ PUNS

Exercise 1

In this interview, Robert Armstrong explains the origin of the name ***couch potato***. He makes two puns in his explanation. A ***pun*** is a play on words to make people laugh. It is formed by using words that sound alike or words that have more than one meaning. Read the two examples of puns:

Type A—Words That Sound Alike

Example:	"What is black and white and *red* all over?"
Answer:	"A newspaper."
Explanation:	***Red*** is the same sound as ***read***, the past participle of ***to read***.

Type B—Words That Have More Than One Meaning

Example:	"What has four wheels and *flies*?"
Answer:	"A garbage truck."
Explanation:	***Flies*** can mean "goes through the air" (verb), or it can mean "insects" (noun).

Listen to this segment of the interview. Then discuss the two puns with a partner.

ARMSTRONG:

We as Couch Potatoes beckon people to "come out of the closet," and claim it loud that they are a "tuber and proud." The "tuber" part of it is one of the reasons why we selected the potato to be our icon, because it is, after all, ***a tuber*** and has many ***eyes***.

INTERVIEWER:

Oh, I just got it—as in "tube."

ARMSTRONG:

Yes, watching the tube, and all the eyes of the potato used to watch TV with. It just seemed like a good symbol for us to rally around.

EXPLANATION

Robert Armstrong is making a pun when he talks about a ***tuber*** with many ***eyes***. This is a Type B pun. He is playing with the two meanings of these words:

1. The potato comes from the ***tuber*** family (a type of underground root). Television is frequently called "the ***tube***" because it has an electronic tube inside. Therefore, a person who watches TV is humorously called "a ***tuber***."

2. The potato has ***eyes*** (marks on the potato that are called "eyes") and we use our ***eyes*** to watch TV.

Exercise 2

Puns are often used in jokes. Work with another student. Discuss the three choices for each joke. Choose the answer that makes a pun and try to explain the play on words. Then decide whether it is an example of a Type A or Type B pun. The first one has been done for you.

B 1. What did the mayonnaise say to the refrigerator?

    a. It's too cold in here! I'm freezing.

    (b.) Close the door! I'm dressing.

    c. Let me out! It's time to eat.

Explanation: "Dressing" has two meanings: 1) putting clothes on (verb) and 2) a sauce that is put on salad (noun).

_____ 2. Why is a baseball team like a good pancake?

    a. It has to have a good batter.

    b. They both run a lot.

    c. It has to have good players.

_____ 3. My doctor put me on a seafood diet, and now I only eat when . . .

    a. I can have lobster.

    b. I see food.

    c. I go fishing.

_____ 4. Why are chefs mean?

    a. because they heat the butter and stir the sauce

    b. because they beat the eggs and whip the cream

    c. because they grease the pans and bake the bread

_____ 5. How do you know that robbers are really strong?

    a. They lift weights.

    b. They break into safes.

    c. They hold up banks.

(continued on next page)

_____ 6. What did the ocean say to the shore?

    a. Nothing; it just waved.

    b. It asked it to move closer.

    c. It told it to stay dry.

_____ 7. What is a protein?

    a. a chemical substitute for meat

    b. someone interested in sports

    c. someone in favor of teenagers

_____ 8. Why was the baseball player arrested?

    a. because they found him drinking at home

    b. because they caught him stealing bases

    c. because they found him throwing things

_____ 9. Why does John always wear a wristwatch?

    a. He likes to take his time.

    b. He has a busy schedule.

    c. He doesn't want to lose it.

_____ 10. What are the strongest days?

    a. Monday and Tuesday. They're after the weekend.

    b. Saturday and Sunday. All the rest are weekdays.

    c. Wednesday and Thursday. They fall in the middle.

Exercise 3

*Puns are also used in advertising. Look at each ad. Try to explain the pun.
Then determine what type of pun it is.*

**ITS POWER WILL MOVE YOU.
ITS BEAUTY WILL STOP YOU.
The new Taylor sports car**

Word Processing
anybody can
pick up.

Schneider's Jewelers

Carats are
great for
your eyes.

**Hanson's
Laptop**

8 FOLLOW-UP ACTIVITIES

DISCUSSION QUESTIONS

In groups, discuss your answers to the following questions.

1. Do you agree with Robert Armstrong that watching TV helps "keep the
peace" among family members? Does your family have difficulty
deciding what to watch on TV? How does your family decide what to
watch?

(continued on next page)

2. Do you agree that "if it's on TV, it must be good"? Do you agree that most TV programming is good? In your opinion, are there any shows that should *not* be on television? Or would you censor any programs in your own home? If so, which ones?

▨ ESSAY TOPICS

Choose one of the following topics.

1. Write a letter to the "Couch Potato" newsletter. Tell the readers of the newsletter what you think of their club and the idea of couch potatoes.

2. Do you suffer from "intellectual guilt" about how much TV you watch? Write an essay in which you express your feelings about the quantity and quality of TV that you watch.

▨ DEBATE: HOW MUCH TV?

A. Taking Notes to Prepare

*Listen to the interview again. Take notes on Robert Armstrong's humorous arguments in favor of couch potatoes. An example has been provided for you. Use these notes to help you review and prepare the pros and cons of unlimited TV viewing in the **debate** on page 37.*

Robert Armstrong's arguments in favor of couch potatoes:

gets the family together

_____

_____

_____

_____

_____

_____

_____

B. Debate

For this debate, the class is divided into two teams. The debate will focus on whether or not TV viewing should be limited.

Team A will argue in favor of unlimited TV viewing.

> You believe that people should watch as much TV as they like. You will argue that people get a lot of important information from television and that watching TV is a good form of relaxation. You also think that TV is the quickest way to find out what is happening in today's busy world.

Team B will argue in favor of limiting TV viewing.

> You believe that people should limit their TV viewing to one hour a day. You will argue that television creates unnecessary desires. You think that TV teaches values that are not good. You also think TV creates passivity in people.

Prepare your arguments. A moderator will lead the debate.

DEBATE PROCEDURES

Team A begins with a three-minute presentation.

Team B then gives a three-minute presentation.

Team A responds to Team B's presentation for three minutes.

Team B responds to Team A's presentation for three minutes.

After the debate, the moderator evaluates the strength of both arguments.

"A Couch Potato" was first broadcast on *Morning Edition*, December 27,1987. The interviewer is Susan Stamberg.

THE BIBLE HOSPITAL

PREDICTING

From the title, discuss what you think the interview is about.

2 | THINK AHEAD

In groups, discuss your answers to the following questions.

1. Do you have anything that you would never throw away? Might someone else throw it away? Why do you keep it?

2. Do you have any special books? What books get used the most in your home?

3. Do your parents expect you to do the same work they did? Why or why not? How will your work life be different from theirs?

3 | VOCABULARY

Read the following sentences. The highlighted words will help you understand the interview. Try to guess the meaning of these words from the context of the sentences. Then write a synonym or your own definition of the words.

1. Today it's often cheaper to buy a new pair of shoes than to **restore** an old pair.

   _____

2. The dictionary was so old and used so often that it began to fall apart, and he had to **rebind** it.

   _____

3. She was old and poor, and her clothes were **worn** from living on the street for so long.

   _____

4. Her favorite cookbook had been opened and closed so often that the **spine** was broken, and pages were falling out.

   _____

(continued on next page)

5. Many people will keep old photographs or objects for years just for *sentimental* reasons.

    _____

6. To become members of the church, their children had to be *baptized*.

    _____

7. It was not until *confirmation*, however, that her children officially promised their loyalty to the church.

    _____

8. The coffee he spilled left a *stain* on his white shirt.

    _____

9. Before she left on her trip to Italy, she asked her Italian friend for some *tips* on which sights to see there.

    _____

10. Since his wife *passed away* two years ago, he has lived alone with his dog.

    _____

11. With so much more free time in later life, many people take up new hobbies after they *retire*.

    _____

Now try to match the words with a definition or synonym. Then compare your answers with those of another student. The first one has been done for you.

_b_	1. restore	a.	a dirty or colored spot
___	2. rebind	b.	bring back into use
___	3. worn	c.	died
___	4. spine	d.	suggestions
___	5. sentimental	e.	accepted as a member of a Christian church after a religious ceremony in which the person is purified with holy water

_____ 6. baptized

_____ 7. confirmation

_____ 8. stain

_____ 9. tips

_____ 10. passed away

_____ 11. retire

f. having tender feelings

g. put papers together again and put into a cover

h. give up one's work

i. showing signs of being used; old

j. a religious ceremony in which a person obtains full membership in a Christian church

k. structure that holds a book together

4   TASK LISTENING

Listen to the interview. Find the answer to the following question.

Which type of book, besides the Bible, is mentioned in this interview?

5   LISTENING FOR MAIN IDEAS

Listen to the interview again. The interview has been divided into four parts, each expressing a main idea. You will hear a beep at the end of each part. As you listen, circle the answer that best expresses the main idea in that part. Compare your answers with those of another student.

PART 1   What does Patrick Kirby do?

     a. He works in a hospital.

     b. He works in a book-repair shop.

     c. He works in a library.

PART 2   How does Kirby restore a book?

     a. He keeps all the book's leather.

     b. He replaces all the book's leather.

     c. He adds some new leather to the book.

(continued on next page)

PART 3 Why do people get their old books restored?

a. because the old books have a special meaning

b. because new books are more expensive

c. because the old books have stains

PART 4 What is true about the Kirby family bookbinding business?

a. The business has always sewn books by hand.

b. Three generations have been involved in the business.

c. The family business may die.

6 | LISTENING FOR DETAILS

*Read the statements for Part 1. Then listen to Part 1 again and decide whether the statements are true or false. As you listen, write a **T** or **F** next to each statement. Compare your answers with those of another student. If you disagree, listen again to Part 1.*

PART 1

_____ 1. Patrick Kirby owns the Bible Hospital.

_____ 2. He does much of his work by hand.

_____ 3. He restores mostly private books.

_____ 4. Twenty percent of his work is rebinding bibles.

_____ 5. He restores about fifty large leather-bound bibles each year.

Repeat the same procedure for Parts 2–4.

PART 2

_____ 6. Kirby will have to completely resew the book he's holding.

_____ 7. The pages of the book are still together.

_____ 8. The spine of the book is split.

_____ 9. The old spine will be thrown away.

PART 3

_____ 10. Hand bibles are expensive.

_____ 11. People often have dates written in their bibles.

_____ 12. The dates often reflect an important religious ceremony.

_____ 13. People get their cookbooks restored because old cookbooks were of better quality.

_____ 14. People want to preserve their checkmarks and tips in cookbooks.

PART 4

_____ 15. Kirby's father died in the sixties.

_____ 16. The Kirby family business has been going since 1935.

_____ 17. Some of Kirby's equipment is as old as he is.

_____ 18. Hand sewing a book would take about one hour.

_____ 19. Hand-sewn jobs are better than machine-sewn jobs.

_____ 20. Kirby will probably sell the business when he retires.

7 LOOKING AT LANGUAGE

■ PREFIXES

Exercise 1

Listen to the following sentences from the interview. What is the meaning of the prefix **re-** in each of the italicized words?

1. He's a **restorer** of books and he does much of the work by hand.

2. He **restores** books mostly for libraries, but about 20 percent of his work is **rebinding** private books, mainly bibles.

3. This one has to be **resewed***, completely **resewed**.

4. This piece of leather here will be lifted off the board here, pulled back about an inch or so, then we'll **reinsert** a new piece of leather in here.

*can also be "resewn"

(continued on next page)

EXPLANATION

In the examples on page 43, **re-** means "again." Prefixes are common in English. They are sometimes added to the front of a word to change its meaning. For example, notice how the prefix **re-** adds the meaning of "again" to the following words:

> **re**do   **re**make   **re**establish   **re**unite

Exercise 2

What follows is a list of twelve common prefixes in English. Write the meaning of each prefix in the blank space. Choose from the definitions listed at the end of the exercise. Use the sample words to help you find the meaning. The first one has been done for you. Compare your answers with those of another student. Then, together, add other words you know with the same prefix.

PREFIX	DEFINITIONS	SAMPLE WORDS
1. **bi-**	*twice or two*	bicentennial; bilingual
		_____
2. **contra-**	_____	contradict; contraception
		_____
3. **de-**	_____	defrost; depopulate
		_____
4. **dis-**	_____	disagree; disorder
		_____

5. **en- (em-)** _____   enlist; empower

_____

6. **in-**   _____   infinite; illiterate;

   (il-; im-; ir-)   impossible; irregular

_____

7. **inter-**   _____   international; interracial

_____

8. **mis-**   _____   mistrust; misconduct

_____

9. **pre-**   _____   premature; prerecorded

_____

10. **uni-**   _____   university; unisex

_____

DEFINITIONS

one; the same   not

reverse; undo   put in, on

against   twice or two

bad; wrong   between

before   stop; refuse

Exercise 3

Read the following sentences. Decide which prefix is appropriate for the form and meaning of the given root word. Consider the information from the interview and the context of the sentence.

1. The fact that Kirby's business may die may be a _____ lateral decision, because both he and his children have already decided that they won't continue in his business.

    a. uni-   b. bi-

2. Many of the books that Kirby works with are _____ composed because they are so old.

    a. pre-   b. de-

3. The spine of a book that needs rebinding is usually_____ connected from the rest of the book.

    a. inter-   b. dis-

4. Perhaps one of the reasons people go to the Bible Hospital is that their books are _____ replaceable.

    a. ir-   b. in-

5. According to the interviewer, cookbooks are _____ dangered if they live in kitchens.

    a. en-   b. in-

6. When someone brings a book to Kirby, he or she has probably _____ determined that it is for sentimental reasons.

    a. uni-   b. pre-

7. People are rarely _____ satisfied with the work done at the Bible Hospital because Kirby puts so much care into repairing old books.

    a. in-   b. dis-

8. In Kirby's work, a book may have to be _____ sected in order to put a new spine in it.

    a. bi-   b. inter-

9. A bookbinder tries to make a book look _____ form again, matching new leather with the old.

               a. contra-   b. uni-

10. Children may _____ understand the importance of maintaining a family business.

               a. mis-   b. dis-

8   FOLLOW-UP ACTIVITIES

▓ DISCUSSION QUESTIONS

In groups, discuss your answers to the following questions.

1. What kinds of possessions do you save? What kinds of things do you throw away? Give examples.

2. Some trades and professions are dying because children no longer continue their family's business. Give examples of dying trades and professions in your country.

▓ ESSAY TOPICS

Choose one of the following topics.

1. Describe something that you feel sentimental about. Why does it have a special place in your heart? Write an essay in which you describe your feelings.

2. What is the ideal relationship between people and their work? Is it preferable to work in more anonymous or impersonal settings, such as in a large corporation? Or is it preferable to work in more traditional or personal settings, such as in a family business? Write an essay in which you express your opinion.

◼ CASE STUDY: THE ZIMO FAMILY

A. Taking Notes to Prepare

By focusing on some of the issues presented in the interview, you may be better able to discuss the pros and cons of children continuing their family's business in the follow-up **case study** on pages 49–50.

Listen to the interview again. Take notes on Patrick Kirby's bookbinding business. Key phrases and some examples have been provided for you.

What Kirby's business gives people:

sentimental value

The similarities between Kirby's business today and his father's business in 1939:

the stamper

The future of Kirby's business:

children aren't interested

B. Case Study

You have listened to Patrick Kirby describe his bookbinding business. His business will probably not continue because his children have no interest in it.

Work in groups. Read the following case study. Discuss what decision Mike should make about his father's business. Try to reach an agreement. Take notes on your group's discussion. Then compare your opinion with those of the other groups.

The Zimo family has been in the hardware business for three generations. In the 1930s Michael Zimo's father opened the first hardware store in a small town in New Jersey. The store was very successful, and after his father passed away, Michael took over the business.

Michael has run the hardware store since 1952. The business has been prosperous, and he is well respected in the community. Two of his brothers have helped out with the business over the years. As his children, Mike Jr. and Donna, grew up, they also helped out in the store. Michael always thought that his son, Mike Jr., would eventually take over the family business.

After high school, Michael's children went away to college. Mike Jr. went to Boston College and majored in music. He dreamed of making it as a musician. While at college, he played the guitar in a local band. Unfortunately, he had trouble keeping up with his studies and had to drop out of college before completing his degree. When this happened, Mike's father persuaded him to come home and help out with the family business.

Mike decided to accept his father's offer, left Boston and his band, and went home to work with his father. The business was thriving, and he did enjoy the benefits of working with his family. He could take time off when he needed; he could work a fairly flexible schedule. Two years later, he got married and bought a house. His job enabled him to pay the mortgage on the house. Mike enjoyed working at the family hardware store, but somehow he felt unsettled: He had never fulfilled his dream of becoming a musician.

(continued on next page)

When Michael Sr. turned sixty-two, he was diagnosed with cancer. His doctors told him he probably had six months or less to live. Preparing for his death, he talked to his son about continuing the family business, but Mike's response wasn't totally positive. He felt conflicted. He wanted to support his father, but he couldn't imagine working at the hardware store all his life. He told his father that he didn't want to have to wait on customers all his life. He still wanted to pursue his music career. He also wanted to "make it on his own."

Mike's father couldn't believe that his son didn't care about the family business, the business he himself had dedicated his life to. He was hurt and disappointed that his son could abandon him. He was proud of what he had built and wanted his business to continue serving the community after he was gone. He also couldn't understand how his son could give up such a secure position. There was a lot of money to be made in this business. If Mike took the risk of pursuing a career in music, he might not succeed. And what's certain is that the family business would die.

Mike thought about his father's point of view; he didn't want to disappoint his father. But, at the same time, he wanted to pursue his own goals, to do something different. When he told his father that he felt frustrated that he had never really pursued his dream of becoming a musician, his father responded, "You gotta do what you gotta do."

"The Bible Hospital" was first broadcast on *All Things Considered*, April 27, 1994. The interviewer is Linda Wertheimer.

A Boy's Shelter
for Street People

1   **PREDICTING**

From the title, discuss what you think the interview is about.

| **2** | # THINK AHEAD |

Work in groups. Read the following statements. Do you agree with them? See if everyone in your group has the same opinion.

1. Society must help the people who have no homes and live on the street.

2. Most people who live on the street are there because they don't want to work.

3. You can usually tell what people are like by the way they look.

4. Most people who live on the street have mental problems.

| **3** | # VOCABULARY |

The following words will help you understand the interview. Try to guess the meaning of the words. Use your knowledge of English, or use your dictionaries. In each set of words, cross out the word that does not have a similar meaning to the highlighted word. Then compare your answers with those of another student. Discuss why these words are similar. The first one has been done for you.

1. **homeless**	street people	~~wealthy people~~	poor people
2. **startling**	amazing	calming	surprising
3. **resisted**	relented	opposed	fought
4. **impressionable**	affected by others	wise	easily influenced
5. **donation**	salary	gift	contribution
6. **volunteer**	help	charge	offer
7. **commitment**	comprehension	duty	obligation
8. **unconditionally**	politically	freely	without expectation

| 9. **threatening** | frightening | caring | scary |
| 10. **campaign** | drive | religion | effort |

---

4 | TASK LISTENING

Listen to the interview. Find the answer to the following question.

> Who is interviewed with Trevor?

---

5 | LISTENING FOR MAIN IDEAS

Listen to the interview again. The interview has been divided into four parts, each expressing a main idea. You will hear a beep at the end of each part. As you listen, circle the answer that best expresses the main idea in that part. Compare your answers with those of another student.

PART 1   What did Trevor Ferrell do when he learned about the homeless?

    a   He asked his parents if he could live in the city.

    b. He asked the newspaper to write about the homeless.

    c. He tried to help the homeless.

PART 2   What did Trevor and his father learn about street life?

    a. They found out that the homeless do not want to work.

    b. They found out that living on the street is very hard.

    c. They found out that street life is not so bad.

PART 3   How does the community help the homeless?

    a. People bring them food in vans.

    b. The homeless stay with families.

    c. The community helps them find jobs.

(continued on next page)

PART 4   What has happened to Trevor because of his work with the
homeless?

     a. He has more fun.

     b. His attitude has changed.

     c. He is more tired.

6   LISTENING FOR DETAILS

*Read the questions for Part 1. Then listen to Part 1 again. As you listen,
circle the best answer. Compare your answers with those of another
student. If you disagree, listen again to Part 1.*

PART 1

1. When did Trevor first realize that people were living on the streets of
Philadelphia?

     a. two years ago

     b. in November

     c. twelve months ago

2. How did Trevor learn about the homeless?

     a. from friends in the suburbs

     b. from his parents

     c. from a news report

3. How did Trevor's parents react when he wanted to go to the city to
help someone?

     a. They were amazed.

     b. They thought it was a great idea.

     c. They were angry.

4. What did Trevor give to a man on the street?

   a. a blanket and pillow

   b. a note saying "God bless you"

   c. food

5. What happened after Trevor's story was published?

   a. The local paper donated money.

   b. People volunteered to help.

   c. Trevor wrote a book.

Repeat the same procedure for Parts 2–4.

PART 2

6. Which is **not** a name of Trevor's street friends?

   a. Chico

   b. Ralph

   c. Big Joel

7. What is **not** mentioned as a reason why people live on the street?

   a. They lost their jobs.

   b. They have mental problems.

   c. They are dirty.

8. How long did Trevor and his father stay on the street?

   a. a few minutes

   b. a few hours

   c. a few days

9. What happened when Trevor and his father tried to stay on the street?

   a. They were cold, so they went home.

   b. They were cold, but they slept in sleeping bags.

   c. They were cold because they slept on the sidewalk.

(continued on next page)

10. How did Trevor and his father feel about their night on the street?

    a. proud

    b. not proud

    c. angry

11. What does Trevor's father think about the people living on the street?

    a. He thinks they're crazy.

    b. He doesn't think they have such a difficult life.

    c. He doesn't understand how they can live there.

PART 3

12. Who donates food to the homeless?

    a. fast-food chains

    b. hospital coordinators

    c. the families of the homeless

13. Who pays for the food for the homeless?

    a. The homeless pay.

    b. No one pays.

    c. The city of Philadelphia pays.

14. What do the homeless need most?

    a. caring

    b. clothing

    c. food

15. Why do people accept food from Trevor?

    a. because he's a youngster

    b. because he can help them to get a job

    c. because he is threatening

PART 4

16. How has Trevor's life changed?

    a. He is not allowed to play with his friends as much.

    b. He is not able to play with his friends as much.

    c. He does not want to play with his friends as much.

17. How does Trevor feel about the change?

    a. It's worth it.

    b. He wishes he could help more.

    c. He is grateful for his new life.

18. What has Trevor learned from his experience?

    a. People are scary.

    b. People are nice.

    c. You should treat people according to the way they look.

19. How is the money from the book *Trevor's Place* used?

    a. His mother uses it for the family.

    b. It is used for Trevor's campaign.

    c. Trevor will use it for his college education.

7 LOOKING AT LANGUAGE

▓ PASSIVE VOICE

Exercise 1

Listen again to Trevor's father describe how food is given to the homeless. Focus on the verbs in boldface italics. Discuss who you think is doing these things.

(continued on next page)

The vans go in every night serving homeless people food—food that's generously **donated** by fast-food chains, and there are volunteer coordinators of the effort, individual families. There are over a hundred families in the Philadelphia area that cook on a regular basis, and food **is taken in** and **given** freely, unconditionally to people that are on the streets and obviously have a need for someone, so much more of a need for the caring that's exchanged than really the food, I guess.

EXPLANATION

In the three examples above, the focus is on the "food" rather than on the person or thing that does something with the food. We use the passive voice when we want to emphasize the "receiver" of the action rather than the person or thing that does the action. Trevor's father chose to focus on "food" rather than on the person or thing that was donating it, taking it in, or giving it away.

The passive voice, in any tense, is formed by the verb **to be** and the past participle. The person or thing that does the action is not always mentioned in the passive voice. When it is mentioned, it is introduced with the word **by.** Notice the verb form and the use of **by** in each example:

Food **is** generously **donated by** fast-food chains.
Food **is taken in.** (**by** volunteers)
Food **is given** freely. (**by** volunteers)

Exercise 2

Practice using the passive voice. Change the following sentences from active to passive voice. Be sure to use the same verb tense as in the original sentence. The first one has been done for you.

1. Fast-food chains donate food to the homeless.

   Food is donated to the homeless by fast-food chains.

2. Volunteers give free food to the homeless.

   _____

3. Trevor helped the homeless.

   _____

4. A journalist interviewed Trevor.

   _____

5. Homeless people named the shelter "Trevor's Place."

   _____

Exercise 3

Read the following news story about Trevor's campaign for the homeless. Decide whether the focus is on the person or thing that does the action (active voice) or on the person or thing that receives the action (passive voice).

Complete the story with the verbs in parentheses. Use the active or passive voice in the simple past tense. The first two have been done for you.

New Shelter for City's Homeless

Many programs have recently been developed to help the city's homeless population. Perhaps the most interesting program is an eleven-year-old boy's campaign to help Philadelphia's homeless.

Two years ago, eleven-year-old Trevor Ferrell and his parents, Frank and Janet Ferrell, ____*put*____ (put) an ad in a local paper asking for donations to help Philadelphia's homeless. The paper was interested in finding out what Trevor and his parents were doing. Later that week, Trevor ___*was interviewed*___ (interview) by the paper, and his story _____ (publish). After the publication of that story, many people _____ (send) donations for the homeless to Trevor and his family. Food _____ (donate) by fast-food chains. Many people

(continued on next page)

_____ (volunteer) to help Trevor and his family. Someone
         6

even _____ (contribute) a van. Volunteers _____
            7   8

(start) to give out free food to people living on the streets.

   But Trevor Ferrell's campaign did not stop there. Last week, a

permanent shelter for the homeless _____ (open). Now many
                                                  9

of Philadelphia's homeless have a warm place to shower and sleep.

Through his hard work, Trevor has become friends with many of the

homeless people. The people know and love him. In fact, the shelter

_____ (name) "Trevor's Place" by the people who stay there.
         10

8 | FOLLOW-UP ACTIVITIES

▨ DISCUSSION QUESTIONS

In groups, discuss your answers to the following questions.

1. If you were Trevor's parents, would you support him in helping
   homeless people? Why or why not?

2. In your opinion, is it anyone's responsibility to take care of the
   homeless? If so, whose? Family members of the homeless? Volunteer
   families in the community? The city? The state? Others?

▨ ESSAY TOPICS

Choose one of the following topics.

1. Trevor said that his experience with the homeless had changed his life
   completely. Have you ever had an experience that changed your life
   completely? Write an essay in which you discuss this experience.

2. Is Trevor's story a typical one? Have people's attitudes toward the
   homeless changed over the years? If so, how and why?

▤ CASE STUDIES: PROFILES OF THE HOMELESS

A. Taking Notes to Prepare

By focusing on some of the descriptions and feelings about the homeless that have been discussed in the interview, you may have a better background for analyzing the material in the follow-up **case studies** on pages 62–65.

Listen to the interview again. Take notes on Trevor's story. Key phrases and some examples have been provided for you.

Street people's reactions to Trevor's kindness:

said "God bless you"

_____

_____

_____

_____

Trevor's feelings about the people living on the street:

he wanted to do something for them right away

_____

_____

_____

_____

Reasons why people live on the street:

some lost their jobs

_____

_____

_____

_____

B. Case Studies

You have listened to some reasons why people live on the street. Now you will read some character profiles of homeless people in New York City. You will analyze the homeless situation based on these profiles.

Work in groups of five. Each person in the group will choose one of the profiles and prepare to give information about that person to the rest of the group. As you read, fill in the chart on page 65 with information from the profile. Then interview the others in your group. Use the chart to help you talk about the profile. Complete the rest of the chart as you listen to each other's descriptions.

After you fill in the information, use the chart to analyze and discuss the homeless situation. Follow the analyzing procedure on page 65.

DONALD

Donald has a neat appearance. He looks different from the rest of the men in the shelter where he stays. His eyes are clear; his appearance is neat; but he looks frightened.

Donald is twenty-nine and represents a new type of homeless person. He is able to work but has been forced onto the streets because he lost his job and can't find an apartment he can afford to rent.

A quiet, slender man, Donald worked for six years in a photography lab. When the company was sold to new owners, they fired more than half the employees. Since then, he has been trying to find work. He fills out application after application, but he can't get a job.

Four weeks ago, Donald lost his apartment. His unemployment money ran out. He has been on the streets ever since. He is trying to get welfare money, but he needs a permanent address where he can receive necessary documents. Without the documents, he cannot get welfare.

Donald comes from a religious family. He was taught to be kind to everyone, but he can't tolerate the life of the shelter; many of the people there are drug addicts and alcoholics. He can't sleep at night because he sees people taking drugs. He feels like he's going crazy.

Donald has no wife or children. His other relatives are living in the South. He doesn't want them to know how far he's fallen. He wants to get out of this situation. He's sure there is a better life for him somewhere.

FLORENCE

Florence, forty-three, a big, broad woman, wears an evening dress and a fake white fur coat. She is five months pregnant. She is not sure who the father of her baby is. She says that she'll know when the baby is born. She says she'll keep the baby if it's a girl. She has eight other children by three former husbands. Her last husband was more than eighty years old.

Florence has been homeless for three years, on and off. She spent time in Los Angeles trying to be an actress, but she was not very successful. She also spent time in a mental institution seven or eight years ago.

Florence keeps her possessions in a locker in the downtown bus station. She spends her nights in the subways. She likes it in the subways because she can spend time with friends and talk about the Lord. She says she wants to marry the Lord.

SALLY

Sally is a forty-five-year-old woman. She has one missing tooth and many clothes under her old dark coat, but otherwise she appears to be an ordinary, attractive woman. She is polite and her speech is clear. She carries a shopping bag full of books that she says she reads. In fact, she can intelligently discuss one of the books she is carrying. She says she identifies with some of the characters in the story.

Sally attended twelve years of school and an additional two years at a small-town community college. She has been living on the streets for only six weeks. She got divorced two years ago. Her ex-husband took most of the money after their divorce.

When Sally first came to New York, she lived in cheap hotels until she had no more money. Then she spent many nights in the waiting room of the downtown bus station. Finally she got a job with a food chain, but when she asked for a job transfer, she was fired.

She has two daughters: One is twenty years old, the other is twenty-two. The twenty-two-year-old has an apartment in the city. However, she and Sally don't get along very well, so Sally has decided to live on the street for now. Sometimes she sleeps in the bus station, where it's warm.

Sally tries to keep herself clean. She always carries clean clothes and a toothbrush with her. She takes a shower in one of the city's shelters whenever she can. She never thought she would end up in this situation.

(continued on next page)

GEORGE

George has white hair, a high forehead, and angry eyes. Long ago, he taught physics at one of the city's major universities. Now he is very ill; his speech is unclear. He tells stories that don't make sense. He talks about "angels."

George appears to be in his early fifties. He carries all his things in a plastic shopping bag. His shirt is filthy. He is often infested with lice from sleeping on the streets.

However, a neighborhood church donated some clothes to George. He likes the people at the church and sometimes gets a free dinner there. People say that when he goes to the church he sometimes thinks clearly.

George spends many of his nights on a park bench. Sometimes he sits in an all-night cafe, when he has enough money for a few cups of coffee. When he hasn't eaten in a while, the waiter in the cafe will usually give him something to eat on credit.

JEAN

Jean, thirty-nine, spends sleepless nights walking around the neighborhood where she grew up. She enters buildings and looks through garbage to see if she can find clothes. Several years ago, she and her mother lost their home; the apartment building they lived in was burned down.

Jean was born mentally retarded. Yet the way she speaks gives the impression of normal intelligence. Jean's mother was an alcoholic. She died of cancer about four years ago, and Jean has been homeless ever since.

Jean is a large woman. Her dark gray hair is freshly washed. It is important for her to stay clean. She doesn't want to smell like some of the other women in the subway. Jean often goes to a day shelter where she can get a shower and a meal.

Jean finishes her wandering every morning at six o'clock in a diner where the owner sometimes gives her two dollars. She tries to pay the owner back at the beginning of the month, when she receives her social security check.

	Age	Education	Job Experience	Present Housing Situation	Psychological Profile	Family Background
Donald						
Florence						
Sally						
George						
Jean						

Analyzing Procedure

1. Compare and contrast the information you have categorized on the chart. Can you find any similarities or differences?

2. Try to characterize the homeless population. Can you make generalizations about who these people are? Are there any characteristics that make it difficult to generalize?

3. Reevaluate your ideas or opinions about homeless people. Look at the statements on page 52 under *Think Ahead*. Do you have the same opinions about these statements as before? Discuss whether or not any of them have changed.

4. Analyze further. Find out more about the homeless. Where can you get further information?

"A Boy's Shelter for Street People" was first broadcast on *Morning Edition*, November 30, 1985. The interviewer is Lynn Neary.

THE FOUR NEW FOOD GROUPS

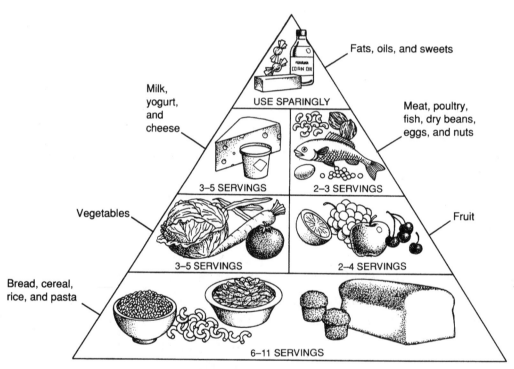

Fats, oils, and sweets

Milk, yogurt, and cheese

USE SPARINGLY

Meat, poultry, fish, dry beans, eggs, and nuts

3–5 SERVINGS

2–3 SERVINGS

Vegetables

Fruit

3–5 SERVINGS

2–4 SERVINGS

Bread, cereal, rice, and pasta

6–11 SERVINGS

Source: U. S. Dept. of Agriculture

1   PREDICTING

From the title, discuss what you think the interview is about.

2   THINK AHEAD

In groups, discuss your answers to the following questions.

1. What are food groups? Do doctors recommend groups of food you should eat? Which ones? Do you follow these recommendations? Why or why not?

2. Have people's diets changed in your country in the last few years? If so, how?

3. Have you recently changed your habits in any way to lead a healthier life? If so, how?

3   VOCABULARY

Read the following sentences. The highlighted words will help you understand the interview. Try to guess the meaning of these words from the context of the sentences. Then write a synonym or your own definition of the words.

1. The United States Constitution is unusual in that it has basically been *unchallenged* since it was written.

   _____

2. Many people have stopped eating deep-fried foods because they are concerned about the level of *cholesterol* in their body.

   _____

3. Preparing fresh peas for dinner is a long process because you have to take them out of the *pod* before cooking them.

   _____

4. The bones of some women break easily as they age because they develop *osteoporosis* in later life.

   _____

(continued on next page)

5. Is it enough to **moderate** our fat consumption, or do we need to go on completely fat-free diets?

_____

6. Children are told to drink milk to build **calcium** in their bones.

_____

7. Protein, a body-building substance found in meat, does not build strong bones. It **leeches** calcium out of the bones.

_____

8. Many people now buy **leaner** cuts of meat because they are concerned about fat.

_____

9. Food companies are now **pushing** their products by creating "light" and "fat-free" versions of the same food.

_____

10. To lose weight, doctors do not advise people to **skip** meals but rather to eat the right food three meals a day.

_____

Now try to match the words with a definition or synonym. Then compare your answers with those of another student. The first one has been done for you.

_e_ 1. unchallenged		a.	omit; leave out
____ 2. cholesterol		b.	drains or draws away
____ 3. pod		c.	a chemical element found in bones and teeth
____ 4. osteoporosis			
____ 5. moderate		d.	having less than the usual proportion of fat
____ 6. calcium		e.	unquestioned; unopposed
____ 7. leeches		f.	trying to sell

_____ 8. leaner

_____ 9. pushing

_____ 10. skip

g. reduce or control

h. substance in the body that can block arteries

i. a weakening of the bones

j. green plant in which peas grow

4	**TASK LISTENING**

Listen to the interview. Find the answer to the following question.

> Give an example of a basic food group that would no longer be a food group in the new list.

5	**LISTENING FOR MAIN IDEAS**

Listen to the interview again. The interview has been divided into five parts, each expressing a main idea. You will hear a beep at the end of each part. As you listen, circle the answer that best expresses the main idea. Compare your answers with those of another student.

PART 1   What happened to the four basic food groups?

  a. They added a new food group.

  b. They became three basic food groups.

  c. They were challenged.

PART 2   What might the result be if we eat from the new food groups?

  a. The population will increase.

  b. We will live longer.

  c. We won't have to worry about eating health foods anymore.

(continued on next page)

PART 3   How should people consume protein?

a. We should consume it with a high-meat diet.

b. We should consume less of it for strong bones.

c. We should consume it through dairy products.

PART 4   Why is meat no longer one of the basic food groups?

a. Leaner cuts of meat are now available.

b. Fast-food meat is not good quality.

c. Meat can cause illnesses.

PART 5   Who has already accepted the four new food group proposal?

a. the American Farm Bureau

b. the Department of Agriculture

c. the Physicians Committee for Responsible Medicine

6 | LISTENING FOR DETAILS

Read the questions for Part 1. Then listen to Part 1 again. As you listen, circle the best answer. Compare your answers with those of another student. If you disagree, listen again to Part 1.

PART 1

1. Of the following, which is **not** mentioned as a group that told us to eat something each day from each of the four basic food groups?

   a. our parents

   b. our teachers

   c. health-care workers

2. Which of the following was **not** one of the original basic food groups?

   a. meat

   b. fish

   c. fruits

3. How long did the original food groups remain unchallenged?

   a. thirty-five years

   b. thirty-nine years

   c. forty-five years

Repeat the same procedure for Parts 2–5.

PART 2

4. What is contained in **all** the new food groups?

   a. legumes

   b. cholesterol

   c. fiber

5. Which is **not** an example of grains?

   a. beans

   b. spaghetti

   c. rice

6. Which is **not** an example of a legume food?

   a. beans

   b. peas

   c. pods

PART 3

7. Whose bone density did researchers measure?

   a. menopausal women

   b. postmenopausal women

   c. men with osteoporosis

(continued on next page)

8. If you want to keep calcium in your bones, you should

   a. drink more dairy products.

   b. reduce your protein intake.

   c. lose more urine.

PART 4

9. In the new food groups,

   a. meat should not be eaten.

   b. meat is an optional food.

   c. only leaner cuts of meat should be eaten.

10. How "lean" is the McLean burger at McDonald's?

    a. 45 percent fat content

    b. 49 percent fat content

    c. as low in fat content as vegetables

11. Which illness does Bernard seem most concerned about in relation to fat in the diet?

    a. heart attacks

    b. obesity

    c. breast cancer

12. How many women suffer from breast cancer today?

    a. one out of nine

    b. one out of ten

    c. one out of eleven

13. Why did meat and dairy products go off the four food group list?

    a. They have too much fat in them.

    b. People couldn't digest them easily.

    c. People skipped them in their daily eating habits.

PART 5

14. Who opposes the new food groups?

    a. former Agriculture Secretary John Clark

    b. the U.S. Department of Agriculture

    c. the medical leaders' children

7 | LOOKING AT LANGUAGE

■ PRESENT REAL CONDITIONAL

Exercise 1

Listen to the following sentences from the interview. Focus on the verb forms in boldface italics. What verb tenses are used in both parts of each sentence (if clause and main clause)? Can you explain why?

1. They found that dairy products just **don't** work if the goal **is** to prevent osteoporosis.

2. If we're on a high meat diet, the large amount of protein that people are eating actually **leeches** calcium out of the bones, and it**'s lost** in the urine.

3. If you **reduce** your protein intake, the calcium **stays** in the bones and that's what seems to be more important in maintaining strong bones.

4. If they **skip** them, they**'ll be** healthier.

EXPLANATION

In sentences 1–3, both clauses use the present tense. When we use an **if** clause to talk about general truths, facts, or habits, both the **if** clause and the main clause are written in the present tense.

   *If we **eat** a lot of dairy products, we **increase** our cholesterol.*

(continued on next page)

Note that in these present real conditions that talk about general truths, facts, or habits, *if* can be replaced with ***whenever***:

> ***Whenever*** *we eat a lot of dairy products, we increase our cholesterol.*

In sentence 4, the verb tenses in the two clauses are different. This sentence is an example of a ***real conditional*** sentence. In this type of sentence, both the *if* clause and the main clause refer to something that can possibly happen in the future. The *if* clause is in the present tense and the main clause is in the future tense.

> *If we **stop** eating dairy products, we **will** decrease our cholesterol.*

Exercise 2

Read the following sentences. Decide whether the sentence can be a statement about general truth, fact, or habit or a statement about future possibility. Consider the information presented in the interview and write the correct tense of the verbs.

1. According to our parents and teachers, if we ＿＿＿＿＿＿＿＿
   (eat)

   something each day from each of the four basic food groups, we

   ＿＿＿＿＿＿＿＿ big and strong.
   (grow up)

2. According to Barnard, if population groups ＿＿＿＿＿＿＿ their diet
   (center)

   on the four new food groups, they ＿＿＿＿＿＿＿ years longer.
   (live)

3. Whenever you ＿＿＿＿＿＿＿ a McLean burger at McDonald's, you
   (eat)

   ＿＿＿＿＿＿＿ meat that is 49 percent fat.
   (consume)

4. People believe that if they ＿＿＿＿＿＿＿ dairy products, they
   (consume)

   ＿＿＿＿＿＿＿ strong bones.
   (build)

5. When protein _____ in the human body, calcium
   (be consumed)

   _____ out of the bones.
   (leech)

6. It is a known fact that if you _____ a lot of grains, you
   (eat)

   _____ calcium in your bones.
   (maintain)

7. Statistics show that if you _____ a woman, your chances of
   (be)

   getting breast cancer _____ one in nine.
   (be)

8. If we as adults _____ our habits, our children _____
   (change)   (have)

   a better life.

9. Scientists have shown that if you _____ a lot of meat, you
   (eat)

   _____ having high cholesterol.
   (risk)

---

8 | FOLLOW-UP ACTIVITIES

▓ DISCUSSION QUESTIONS

In groups, discuss your answers to the following questions.

1. Would it be easy to find food from the four new food groups in your country? What are the main groups of food in your country? Would the dietary customs of people in your country allow you to follow the suggestions for the new food groups?

2. What is your reaction to the new basic food group list? Would you accept it, or would you propose different groups? Why?

■ ESSAY TOPICS

Choose one of the following topics.

1. Do you eat the way you want to eat? Is your diet an ideal one? Write an essay in which you compare and contrast your own eating habits with the eating habits you value.

2. Write a letter to the Department of Agriculture. Express your opinion about the new food group proposal. Urge the department to maintain or change the original four food groups: meat, dairy, fruits and vegetables, and bread and cereal.

■ ROLE PLAY: THE FOUR BASIC FOOD GROUPS

A. Taking Notes to Prepare

By reviewing the information presented in the interview, you may have a better background for discussing the pros and cons of new food groups in the follow-up **role play** on pages 77–80.

Listen to the interview again. Take notes on the reasons given for changing the four basic food groups. Key phrases and some examples have been provided for you.

Current four food groups:

meat
_____

_____

_____

_____

Proposed four food groups:

grains
_____

_____

_____

_____

Beliefs about current four food groups:

Dairy products lead to strong bones.

_____

_____

_____

Problems with current four food groups:

dairy:

doesn't work to keep strong bones or prevent

osteoporosis

meat:

Protein leeches calcium out of bones.

_____

_____

_____

_____

Advantages of proposed four food groups:

no cholesterol

_____

_____

_____

B. Role Play

For this role play, the class is divided into three groups. One group will prepare arguments for the American Farm Bureau. Another group will prepare arguments for the Physicians Committee for Responsible Medicine. The final group will prepare questions for the Department of Agriculture. Read the situation. Choose a group, and after a fifteen-minute preparation, begin the discussion. (continued on next page)

THE SITUATION

For more than thirty-five years, Americans have been told that they should eat something each day from the four basic food groups. Both parents and school teachers have encouraged children to eat three balanced meals a day, composed of meat, fruits and vegetables, dairy products, and bread and cereal.

Now doctors and dieticians are concerned that we have been eating the wrong foods all these years. The Physicians Committee for Responsible Medicine (PCRM) has proposed that two of the four food groups be replaced. Instead of eating dairy and meat each day, we should eat grains and legumes.

The Department of Agriculture, a branch of the U.S. government, is responsible for making any changes in the four food groups. Their recommendations would affect the eating habits of most Americans. The Department of Agriculture is reluctant to support this change, because so much of the American diet centers around eating meat and dairy products. Dairy farms and cattle ranches are big industries in the United States. International exports of dairy and meat products bring a lot of money to the United States.

The American Farm Bureau (AFB) is strongly opposed to the idea of changing the four food groups. Their interest is to protect American farms and support their continued growth by lobbying government officials. Many American farms exist only to raise cattle for meat consumption or dairy cows for milk consumption. Any change in the four food groups could significantly lower the income of these farmers.

Medical leaders, however, have united to try to change the concept of the American diet. They feel Americans must change their eating habits dramatically if they want their children to live healthy lives. The PCRM was formed to put pressure on the Department of Agriculture.

Tomorrow, members of the Department of Agriculture will hold a hearing. They have prepared specific questions for the PCRM regarding the proposal to change the four food groups. They will also listen to the AFB's concerns. Then they will make a decision regarding the status of the food groups.

THE ROLES

THE AMERICAN FARM BUREAU

You are an organization that works to protect the American farm business. You pressure the U.S. government to help farmers. You are interested in protecting the farm industry, including exports to other countries. You represent many dairy farmers and cattle ranchers.

THE PHYSICIANS COMMITTEE FOR RESPONSIBLE MEDICINE

You represent a united group of physicians who are pushing for the four new food groups. You are concerned about the health of children. You are disturbed by the increase in cases of heart attacks, obesity, and breast cancer. You want to convince the Department of Agriculture to change the four basic food groups.

THE DEPARTMENT OF AGRICULTURE

You are a branch of the government that oversees the operations of American agriculture. You are concerned with the functions of American farming and its contribution to American society. Food exportation to other countries brings in a lot of money to the United States. You are concerned about continuing the production of foods that can be exported for profit.

PROCEDURE FOR DISCUSSION

1. Students will divide into three groups (the three roles).

2. The Department of Agriculture will meet to prepare questions for both the AFB and the PCRM.

(continued on next page)

3. The AFB will prepare its arguments in favor of maintaining the four food groups.

4. The PCRM will prepare its arguments in favor of changing the four food groups.

5. The Department of Agriculture will conduct a fifteen-to-twenty minute hearing and listen to the arguments of each group. Members of the department will ask questions.

6. The Department of Agriculture will meet independently to make a decision regarding the four food groups. Once the decision is made, it is announced to the class.

"The Four New Food Groups" was originally broadcast on *Morning Edition*, April 9, 1991. The interviewer is Renee Montaigne.

THE DIRTY DOZEN

---

1 | **PREDICTING**

From the title, discuss what you think the interview is about.

2 | THINK AHEAD

In groups, discuss your answers to the following questions.

1. Describe the beaches with which you are most familiar. Are they clean or dirty? Have they changed in any way over the years? If so, how?

2. Is garbage a problem in your country? How is garbage disposed of? Is it easy or difficult to throw things away?

3. Are people in your country more aware of the environment and recycling today than they were ten years ago?

3 | VOCABULARY

The following words will help you understand the interview. Try to guess the meaning of the words. Use your knowledge of English, or use your dictionaries. In each set of words, cross out the word that does not have similar meaning to the highlighted word. Then compare your answers with those of another student. Discuss why these words are similar. The first one has been done for you.

1. **surf**	water	~~rocks~~	waves
2. **comb**	scatter	search thoroughly	hunt for
3. **Styrofoam**	plastic	natural fiber	a chemical product
4. **prevalent**	rare	common	seen everywhere
5. **nuisance**	threat	irritation	bother
6. **tangle up**	push up	mess up	tie up
7. **undertake**	take on	give up	start on
8. **dump**	throw away	throw out	throw up
9. **debris**	trash	litter	compost
10. **fines**	awards	penalties	punishments

4	# TASK LISTENING

Listen to the interview. Find the answer to the following question.

> Give one example of the dirty dozen.

5	# LISTENING FOR MAIN IDEAS

Listen to the interview again. The interview has been divided into five parts, each expressing a main idea. You will hear a beep at the end of each part. As you listen, circle the answer that best expresses the main idea in that part. Compare your answers with those of another student.

PART 1 What do we find on the beach coasts?

    a. Memorial Day tourists

    b. lots of trash

    c. clean beaches

PART 2 What is the debris mostly made of?

    a. medical waste

    b. metal

    c. plastic

PART 3 Why is this product so harmful to marine life?

    a. It causes animals to die.

    b. It causes animals to eat too much food.

    c. It causes seals to move from the north.

(continued on next page)

PART 4   Can we tell who is responsible for dumping the garbage?

    a. Not always; it's very difficult.

    b. Yes; there are twelve groups.

    c. Yes; it's always the cruise ships.

PART 5   Besides killing animals, why is this litter problem so serious?

    a. People are concerned about saving the environment.

    b. It costs so much money to clean up.

    c. Beaches have disappeared.

6   LISTENING FOR DETAILS

*Read the statements for Part 1. Then listen to Part 1 again and decide whether the statements are true or false. As you listen, write a **T** or **F** next to each statement. Compare your answers with those of another student. If you disagree, listen again to Part 1.*

PART 1

_____ 1. On Memorial Day you might find cigarette butts on the beach.

_____ 2. Volunteers came to the United States from Canada, Mexico, Guatemala, and Japan to clean up U.S. beaches.

_____ 3. They picked up 1,200 tons of plastic.

_____ 4. Patty Devonham wrote a report for the Center for Marine Conservation.

Repeat the same procedure for Parts 2–5.

PART 2

_____ 5. Medical waste is the biggest debris problem found along the coasts.

_____ 6. Styrofoam cups are one of the dirty dozen.

_____ 7. A lot of things found on beaches cannot be recycled.

_____ 8. Fifty-four percent of all trash on beaches is plastic.

PART 3

_____ 9. People generally think plastic is harmless.

_____ 10. Animals can get tangled up in debris.

_____ 11. Animals can eat plastics that poison them.

_____ 12. Animals can get full with plastic, so they stop eating.

_____ 13. Each year 35,000 northern fur seals die because they get tangled up.

_____ 14. Many studies of entanglement have been undertaken.

PART 4

_____ 15. It's hard to tell who's responsible for dumping.

_____ 16. Anybody can dump the dirty dozen.

_____ 17. Cruise ships can legally dump their garbage.

PART 5

_____ 18. The Marpol Annex Five treaty controls the dumping of plastics.

_____ 19. The Coast Guard has made the dumping problem a top priority.

_____ 20. Most people are worried about the environment.

_____ 21. Millions of dollars are spent every year to keep tourists coming back to beaches.

_____ 22. Santa Monica, California, spent $1.3 million just to clean up four miles of beach.

<table>
<tr><td>**7**</td><td># LOOKING AT LANGUAGE</td></tr>
</table>

▨ INDIRECT QUESTIONS

Exercise 1

Listen to the following sentence from the interview.

> "So is there any kind of aggressive effort to go after these industries?"

The above question is a direct question. How is a direct question formed? How would the interviewer's question change if he had begun his question with "Could you tell me . . . "?

EXPLANATION

The normal pattern for **yes/no** question formation is:

Verb + Subject		
Is	there	any kind of aggressive effort to go after these industries?

If we asked for the same information with an **indirect question,** we would ask it as follows:

Expression for Indirect Question	+ if +	Subject +	Verb	
Could you tell me	if	there	is	any kind of aggressive effort to go after these industries?

In a direct yes/no question, the subject and the verb are normally inverted. In an indirect yes/no question, however, the regular affirmative word order is used. Note also that *if* is added after the expression for indirect questions. We often use indirect questions when we

- ask for information from people we don't know

- interrupt someone's conversation

- want to be more polite

The following expressions are commonly used in yes/no indirect questions:

Can you tell me . . . ?	Do you know . . . ?
I'd like to know . . .	Tell me . . .
I'd like to find out . . .	Please tell me . . .
I want to ask . . .	Do you remember . . . ?
I wonder . . .	

Exercise 2

Change the following questions into indirect yes/no questions. Then practice your indirect questions in an interview with another student. Use the information you heard in the radio interview to answer the questions.

1. Did volunteers find garbage on the beaches?

   I'd like to know _____.

2. Was the garbage mostly composed of plastic?

   Do you remember _____?

3. Is medical waste the biggest problem on beaches?

   Can you tell me _____?

4. Is Styrofoam one of the dirty-dozen items that litter the beach?

   Please tell me _____.

(continued on next page)

5. Are the things we find on beaches recyclable?

Do you know _____?

6. Does marine life get hurt by plastic?

I want to ask _____.

7. Do fish stop eating and starve when they get entangled?

Tell me _____.

8. Did any northern fur seals die this year?

Do you know _____?

9. Are cruise ships the only boats responsible for the dumping?

I'd like to find out _____.

10. Will beach communities have to spend much money to clean up beaches?

I wonder _____.

8 | FOLLOW-UP ACTIVITIES

■ DISCUSSION QUESTIONS

In groups, discuss your answers to the following questions.

1. Patty Devonham says that the Coast Guard currently enforces fines on those who dump. But, she says, much needs to be done. What would you suggest?

2. What alternatives do cruise ships have for dumping their garbage? What policies have you heard about for disposing of garbage other than dumping in the ocean?

▧ ESSAY TOPICS

Choose one of the following topics.

1. Imagine that your favorite beach has become covered with trash and dead fish. Write a letter to the cruise-ship company you feel is responsible. Complain about their practice of dumping in the ocean.

2. Some towns in the United States have adopted new garbage policies: Residents pay a fixed price for each bag of garbage they leave to be picked up. This policy forces people to think about the amount of garbage they produce. It also gets people to compost some of their garbage.

   Is this a good policy? Do you think people should be forced into changing their habits, or should they find ways to change themselves? Can you make other suggestions for the garbage problem? Write an essay in which you express your opinion.

▧ CONDUCTING A SURVEY: GARBAGE DISPOSAL

A. Taking Notes to Prepare

Listen to the interview again. Take notes on the problem and solutions of garbage disposal. Key phrases and some examples have been provided for you. Use your notes to help develop questions about garbage for the follow-up **survey** *on pages 90–92.*

By focusing on the problems and solutions of garbage disposal, you may be better prepared to conduct the **survey** that follows.

Types of garbage found on beaches:

cigarette butts

_____

_____

_____

_____

_____

_____

_____

(continued on next page)

Problems that garbage can cause:

threatens marine life

_____

_____

_____

_____

Attempts to deal with the garbage problem:

volunteers comb beaches to pick up trash

_____

_____

_____

_____

B. Survey

*Work in groups. Write a questionnaire. Write five **yes/no** questions that will ask people's opinions about the problem of garbage disposal. Ask about alternatives for dumping and about the responsibility of citizens and the government. Try to use indirect questions. Decide where and when you will conduct the survey, how many people you will question, who they will be, and so on.*

*Take notes on the interesting comments that people make. After you take your survey, count the **yes** and **no** responses. The following grid can be used to write your questions, count responses, and record comments. An example has been provided for you.*

Questions	Yes	No	Comments
Example: *Is garbage a problem in your community?*	*HH+ ///*	*//*	*Many things aren't recycled.*
1.			
2.			
3.			
4.			
5.			

ORAL REPORT

When your group meets again, summarize the information you have collected from each question. Prepare an oral report to present to the rest of the class. Be sure to include an introduction to your survey, a summary of the results you have collected, and a conclusion. The conclusion should include your own interpretation of the information you collected.

ORAL PRESENTATION PROCEDURES

1. The first student introduces the group and gives an introduction to the survey that was conducted.

(continued on next page)

2. The next few students present one or two of the questions that were asked, statistics or general responses that were received, and interesting comments that were made by the people who were interviewed. The comments mentioned should help explain why people answered the way they did.

3. The last student concludes the presentation by summarizing the information from the survey, interpreting it, and perhaps reacting to the results. (For example, "We were surprised to learn that most people thought . . . ")

USEFUL WORDS AND PHRASES

When you talk about the people who answered your survey, you can call them:

• interviewees

• respondents

When you report the information you collected, you can begin:

• They agreed that . . .

• They stated that . . .

• They felt that . . .

• They believed that . . .

When you indicate the number of people surveyed, you can say:

• More than half agreed that . . .

• Almost three-quarters said that . . .

• Less than a third said that . . .

• More than 50 percent of the sample stated that . . .

"The Dirty Dozen" was first broadcast on *All Things Considered*, May 25, 1991. The interviewer is Emil Guillermo.

FROM ONE WORLD
TO ANOTHER

PREDICTING

From the title, discuss what you think the interview is about.

| 2 | **THINK AHEAD** |

In groups, discuss your answers to the following questions.

1. Did one of your parents influence your life in any special way? What was his or her influence on you?

2. Do you feel that you are a part of your neighborhood, school, or community? Why or why not?

3. What influences you the most in making choices: your cultural background, your sex, your role in your family?

| 3 | **VOCABULARY** |

The following words will help you understand the interview. Try to guess the meaning of the words. Use your knowledge of English, or use your dictionaries. In each set of words, cross out the word that does not have a similar meaning to the highlighted word. Then compare your answers with those of another student. Discuss why these words are similar. The first one has been done for you.

1.	**poetry**	poem	poet	~~poll~~
2.	**dedicate**	devote	ignore	show thanks
3.	**raise**	bring up	study	educate
4.	**grow up**	produce	mature	develop
5.	**reservation**	area	land	house
6.	**connected to**	a part of	separate from	tied to
7.	**exiled**	removed	separated	joined
8.	**pore over**	glance at	study	look at carefully
9.	**deal with**	manage	neglect	control
10.	**heritage**	from parents	tradition	creation

4	# TASK LISTENING

Listen to the interview. Find the answer to the following question.

> What is Roberta Hill Whiteman's cultural background?

5	# LISTENING FOR MAIN IDEAS

Listen to the interview again. The interview has been divided into four parts, each expressing a main idea. You will hear a beep at the end of each part. As you listen, circle the answer that best expresses the main idea in that part. Compare your answers with those of another student.

PART 1 Why did Roberta Hill Whiteman write the poem, *"Tuni Kwi Athi? Hiatho."*?

a. The Mohawk Indians asked her to.

b. She wanted to thank her father.

c. She wanted to write for the reservation.

PART 2 How does Roberta Hill Whiteman feel about the two worlds she grew up in?

a. They are very different.

b. They are connected.

c. They make one large community.

PART 3 Why does Roberta Hill Whiteman write poetry?

a. Her grandmother asked her to.

b. She can make a lot of money selling books.

c. The language of poetry makes her feel good.

(continued on next page)

PART 4   What is an important symbol in her poetry?

a. nature

b. modern life

c. her father

6 | LISTENING FOR DETAILS

Read the questions for Part 1. Then listen to Part 1 again. As you listen, circle the best answer. Compare your answers with those of another student. If you disagree, listen again to Part 1.

PART 1

1. What does Roberta Hill Whiteman describe in her poem?

a. white horses

b. leaves

c. a new place

2. What else does she write about in her poem?

a. an iced beer

b. an ice bear

c. a nice bird

3. Who did she dedicate the poem to?

a. her father

b. the Oneida Indians

c. her mother

4. When did her father die?

a. when she was very young

b. in the late sixties

c. n the early twenties

Repeat the same procedure for Parts 2–4.

PART 2

5. Where did Roberta Hill Whiteman grow up?

    a. in Wisconsin

    b. ten miles from Green Bay

    c. on the Oneida reservation

6. What does she say about the Oneida reservation?

    a. The people are nice there.

    b. The land is very rich there.

    c. There is a connection with the "long ago" there.

7. What happened to her as a child?

    a. She was exiled from the reservation.

    b. She began to understand the people around her.

    c. She didn't feel connected to the people around her.

PART 3

8. What influences Roberta Hill Whiteman's poetry the most?

    a. her role as a woman, mother, wife, and daughter

    b. the stories that her grandmother wrote

    c. her grandmother's poetry books

9. What does writing poetry do for her?

    a. It helps her to learn a new language.

    b. It helps her to make up her mind.

    c. It helps her to deal with things.

(continued on next page)

10. What did her grandmother make her pay attention to?

    a. her social being

    b. her mother

    c. her voice through poetry

PART 4

11. What does Roberta Hill Whiteman describe in "Overcast Dawn"?

    a. dreams

    b. family

    c. someone's death

12. What is special about her poems?

    a. her description of natural things

    b. her description of her father

    c. her description of the reservation

13. What does the interviewer say about *Star Quilt*?

    a. It is her second collection of poetry.

    b. It is published in Minneapolis.

    c. It is written by Carolyn Forché.

7   LOOKING AT LANGUAGE

▪ POETRY

Exercise 1

Listen to Roberta Hill Whiteman read parts of two of her poems. Fill in the missing words.

I'uni Kwi Athi? Hiatho.

White horses, tails _____, rise from the cedar.

          1

_____ brings the fat crickets,

    2

trembling breeze.

Find that holy place, a _____.

          3

Embers glow like moon _____.

          4

Will you _____ my ear? An ice bear sometimes

      5

lumbers _____.

      6

Your life still gleams, the edge _____.

          7

I never let you _____.

      8

You showed me how under _____ and darkness,

          9

grasses breathe for _____.

          10

Overcast Dawn

This _____ I feel dreams dying.

      11

One trace is this _____

          12

fallen from a gull,

with its _____ shaft,

      13

slight white down,

and long _____ tip

      14

that won't hold _____.

      15

How will you reach me

if all our _____ are dead?

      16

Discussion Questions

Work in groups and answer the following questions.

1. The first poem, *"T'uni Kwi Athi? Hiatho."* was dedicated to Roberta Hill Whiteman's father. She said that she had never had a chance to thank him for raising her. After reading this poem, what do you think she is thanking her father for? What did he teach her?

2. The second poem's title is "Overcast Dawn." **Overcast** is a word we use to describe the sky when it is covered with dark clouds. **Dawn** is the early part of the morning, the first light of the day. Why do you think the poet chose this title for this poem? Why **overcast**? Why **dawn**?

Exercise 2

Examine the language used in the poems. The language of poetry is not the same as the language we hear or read daily. Roberta Hill Whiteman's description of nature creates images. She said in the interview that she found in language ways to express the "pictures in her mind." A poet uses common words in new ways to create these "pictures." For example, in these poems, the word **moon** is used to create an image of the time of day. In other words, **moon** tells us that it is nighttime. Familiar words are placed in unexpected categories to build the pictures of poetry.

Under each category below, list the words from nature and the descriptive verbs that the poet uses in her two poems. One example from each category has been done for you.

Animals and Parts of the Body of an Animal	Plants	Time of Day	Weather	Descriptive Verbs
horses	*cedar*	*moon*	*breeze*	*trembling*

Exercise 3

Write your own poem using descriptive vocabulary from nature. Try to use words from the categories above to describe people, places, events, or feelings.

8 | FOLLOW-UP ACTIVITIES

■ DISCUSSION QUESTIONS

In groups, discuss your answers to the following questions.

1. Have you ever felt that you moved from one world to another? If so, why did you feel this way?

2. Roberta Hill Whiteman's father taught her to listen and pay attention. He influenced her poetry. She also mentions the influence that her grandmother's books had on her.

   How have your parents or other family members influenced you? What influence did books have on you as a child? How did these things contribute to who you are today?

■ ESSAY TOPICS

Choose one of the following topics.

1. In moving from one culture to another, people often feel exiled in their new environment. In your own experience, have you ever felt a loss of "connectedness" to your environment?

   Write an essay in which you describe the situation and how you felt.

2. Roberta Hill Whiteman said that she had never really thanked her father for raising her.

   Write a letter to a person whom you never thanked for something important.

▨ ROLE PLAY: THE RESERVATION

A. Taking Notes to Prepare

By focusing on how the loss of "connectedness" can affect a person's life choices, you may be able to better understand the issues in the follow-up **role play** on pages 103–105.

Listen to the interview again. Take notes on Roberta Hill Whiteman's feelings about life on and off the reservation and her reasons for becoming a poet. Key phrases and some examples have been provided for you.

Feelings about life on the reservation (Oneida):

everything is connected

the people

_____

_____

_____

Feelings about life off the reservation (Green Bay):

exiled

_____

_____

Reasons why she became a poet:

poetry made her feel connected to things

_____

_____

_____

_____

B. Role Play

For this role play, the class is divided into three groups. One group will prepare the point of view of Glenn Ryan, an American Indian. Another group will prepare the points of view of his parents. A third group will prepare the points of view of his grandparents. Read the situation, choose roles, and after a fifteen-minute preparation, begin a family discussion.

THE SITUATION

Glenn Ryan is a native American Indian. He grew up on a reservation in the Southwest of the United States. He has always felt connected to the people there. His family lives on the reservation, and they share their work on the land with other people living there. The sense of community is very strong because the people have a common heritage.

However, life on the reservation has many limitations. For example, when children grow up, they usually leave the reservation if they want to continue their education or find a good job. There isn't much opportunity for them on the reservation.

Glenn Ryan was a very good student in high school. His grades were high. Consequently, he was offered a four-year scholarship to study at Stanford University in California. He has been studying literature and economics in undergraduate school at Stanford for a year now.

Two weeks ago Glenn returned to the reservation for summer vacation. Reality has also returned. Many of his relatives are unemployed and poor. He feels ashamed and helpless because he is studying on a beautiful campus that he can go back to. He feels guilty that he can no longer help his family with their land on the reservation.

Glenn's return home has deeply affected him. He is thinking of not going back to school. He wants to remain on the reservation with his family because he knows that he could help them by working on the land. He could also get a part-time job off the reservation to bring in some extra money. He does not want to see them unhappy. Tomorrow he will talk with his family to decide whether he will return to school or stay and work on the reservation.

THE ROLES

GLENN RYAN

You don't want to travel between two worlds anymore. You don't feel connected to the university community. You feel you have lost your culture and identity at school. The people there are very different from you. You realize that an education is important, but your family is more important to you right now. You think that you can help build the reservation.

GLENN'S PARENTS

You never had the opportunity to go to college. You believe that Glenn should not abandon his education. In your opinion, his education is the only way he can help the Indian culture. You understand Glenn's feelings but want to convince him to go back to school. You believe he will come back to the reservation once he has completed his studies.

GLENN'S GRANDPARENTS

You would like Glenn to come back to live on the reservation. You have seen too many young people leave the reservation; most of them do not come back. Your heritage has suffered over the years. You want Glenn to stay and help build the reservation and make it stronger. The reservation needs more young people on it. You are afraid that if Glenn goes back to school he will never want to come back to live on the reservation. You fear that he will forget his Indian heritage.

PROCEDURE FOR DISCUSSION

Form new groups to include at least one person playing each of the roles.

1. Glenn, his parents, and his grandparents meet. Each person presents his or her point of view to Glenn.

2. Glenn listens and reacts to the suggestions. Glenn's parents and grandparents also try to convince each other of their opinions.

3. After a fifteen- to twenty-minute discussion, Glenn decides whether to go back to school or stay on the reservation.

4. The group then compares Glenn's decision with the decision of the other groups in class.

"**From One World to Another**" was first broadcast on *All Things Considered*, October 24, 1984. The interviewer is Susan Stamberg.

ATTACHED TO CRIME

9

1   PREDICTING

From the title, discuss what you think the report is about.

2 | THINK AHEAD

In groups, discuss your answers to the following questions.

1. Are today's teenagers different from teenagers of years ago? If so, how are they different? Why are they different?

2. Is crime a problem in schools in your country? What kinds of problems are there in the schools? Describe the atmosphere.

3 | VOCABULARY

The following words will help you understand the report. Try to guess the meaning of these words. Use your knowledge of English, or use your dictionaries. In each set of words, cross out the word that does not have a similar meaning to the highlighted word. Then compare your answers with those of another student. Discuss why these words are similar. The first one has been done for you.

1. **menace**	nuisance	threat	~~violence~~
2. **diverse**	similar	different	mixed
3. **committed**	determined	devoted	distracted
4. **conflict**	agreement	dispute	quarrel
5. **mediator**	fighter	negotiator	peacemaker
6. **defuse**	calm	reduce tension in	concentrate on
7. **chilling**	frightening	upsetting	delightful
8. **humungous**	big	tiny	huge
9. **resent**	feel angry	feel praised	feel bitter
10. **banned**	restricted	prohibited	advertised
11. **stiffer**	calmer	stronger	more severe
12. **defiant**	supportive	fearless	bold

4   TASK LISTENING

Listen to the report. Circle the best answer to the following question.

Who is most responsible for solving disputes among students in this school?

a. the police   b. the high school   c. the students
                          principal

5   LISTENING FOR MAIN IDEAS

Listen to the report again. The report has been divided into six parts, each expressing a main idea. You will hear a beep at the end of each part. As you listen, circle the answer that best expresses the main idea in that part. Compare your answers with those of another student.

PART 1   What have many American communities been unable to escape?

a. children taking weapons to school

b. children becoming menaces

c. children escaping their communities

PART 2   What has affected all the children in this report?

a. living in a new suburban area

b. living with examples of crime

c. living with families who don't understand them

PART 3   Why have these teens begun to accept crime as a fact of life?

a. Racial conflicts on the news influence them.

b. They realize that all kids are aggressive today.

c. They experience it all around them.

PART 4   Why is the Wakefield school less violent now?

  a. Security measures have been taken.

  b. Beepers are used to warn people of violence.

  c. Children protect themselves with weapons.

PART 5   Why are gangs formed?

  a. Kids are afraid.

  b. Kids are asked by older kids to join them.

  c. Kids decide to run away from home.

PART 6   How does Koon deal with the crime problem?

  a. with defiance

  b. with worry

  c. with suspicion

6   LISTENING FOR DETAILS

Read the questions for Part 1. Then listen to Part 1 again. As you listen, circle the best answer. Compare your answers with those of another student. If you disagree, listen again to Part 1.

PART 1

1. What are kids packing to take to school?

  a. lunch boxes

  b. weapons

  c. books to read

2. Which magazine or newpaper is *not* mentioned in the introduction?

  a. the *Washington Post*

  b. *Time*

  c. *Newsweek*

(continued on next page)

Repeat the same procedure for Parts 2–6.

PART 2

3. How can Arlington's Wakefield High School be described?

   a. as a typical American public school

   b. as an ethnically diverse school

   c. as bigger than most schools

4. Which is **not** a racial percentage of the student body?

   a. 36 percent Hispanic

   b. 50 percent Asian

   c. 24 percent black

5. How would the students describe themselves?

   a. as working class

   b. as poor

   c. as wealthy

6. What is true about the kids in this report?

   a. They are often in conflict with other students.

   b. They are committed to solving the problem.

   c. They often feel out of control.

7. Which problem is mentioned as an example of crime that has affected their lives?

   a. One student's little brother sells drugs.

   b. One student has been shot.

   c. One student's family knows someone who committed murder.

8. What other incidents of crime have these students been exposed to?

   a. One student was involved in a drive-by.

   b. One student was raped.

   c. One student's mother was robbed.

PART 3

9. How would these kids describe the crime they see?

    a. as chilling

    b. as racial

    c. as normal

10. Which weapon is ***not*** mentioned as one that is used at parties?

    a. a knife

    b. a gun

    c. a club

11. What happens when someone pulls out a gun?

    a. Someone usually gets hurt.

    b. Everybody runs.

    c. Everybody fights.

PART 4

12. How do the kids feel about the security measures that have been used in their school?

    a. They resent some of them.

    b. They would like more metal detectors.

    c. They want more items banned.

13. What is true about Kassen?

    a. He's eighteen years old.

    b. He has attacked other boys in the bathroom.

    c. He doesn't carry weapons.

(continued on next page)

PART 5

14. Why do kids join gangs?

    a. They cannot protect themselves.

    b. They are afraid of the kids in the gang they join.

    c. They like the name of the gang.

15. What do you have to do to be in a gang?

    a. establish rules

    b. follow rules

    c. adopt the rules of the Boy Scouts

16. Which solutions to the crime problem do the kids suggest?

    a. more parental punishment

    b. fewer gangs

    c. more penalties

17. Why do these kids feel attached to crime?

    a. because they like it

    b. because they can't run away from it

    c. because they want to join the criminals

18. What does Kassen think about?

    a. He thinks about moving to another country.

    b. He thinks about joining a gang.

    c. He thinks about getting through life.

PART 6

19. Why do the kids feel defiant toward crime?

    a. They don't live in the worst neighborhoods.

    b. They can't get away from crime.

    c. They feel safe in their houses.

20. What could be heard at the end of this report?

   a. kids with walkie-talkies

   b. security guards with walkie-talkies

   c. suspicious-looking kids in a fight

7 LOOKING AT LANGUAGE

▪ REPORTED SPEECH

Exercise 1

Listen to the introduction to the report again. Underline the three newspaper headlines that are mentioned.

> Only a few years ago, schoolchildren packed lunch boxes, and now more and more of them are packing weapons. We read about it every day. "Crisis of violence, a menace to childhood," says the *Washington Post*. "Violence hits one in four students," reports the *New York Times,* and *Newsweek* declares that "Our children are growing up scared." Surely some communities have escaped the trend, but too many have not. NPR's Lynn Neary visited a high school in Virginia and has this report.

The introduction quotes the headlines directly from newspapers and a magazine. Words are often deleted in headlines. If they had been written in full sentences of reported speech, they would be written as follows:

> The *Washington Post* said that a crisis of violence was a menace to childhood.

> The *New York Times* reported that violence had hit one in four students.

> *Newsweek* declared that our children were growing up scared.

(continued on next page)

EXPLANATION

In reported speech, we often use the past tense for the reporting verbs. Verbs following the reporting verbs are usually changed to past forms; for example, present tense verbs change to past tense, past tense verbs change to past perfect, present perfect becomes past perfect, and present modals become past modals.

Notice the verb tense changes and pronoun change in the following two examples:

Direct quotes

The reporter explained, "They **have been trained** as mediators who **can step** into a dispute and help defuse it before it gets out of control."

The reporter said, "The school principal **asked us** to use only first names, and **we agreed**."

Reported speech

The reporter explained that they **had been trained** as mediators who **could step** into a dispute and help defuse it before it **got** out of control.

The reporter said that the school principal had **asked them** to use only first names and that **they had agreed.**

Exercise 2

Read the following statements from the teenagers in the report. Rewrite them in reported speech. Make the necessary changes from colloquial speech to the written form. The first one has been done for you.

1. "It does affect me because I have a little brother and I'm scared that he's getting on drugs or something."

   One Wakefield student explained that _____*it did affect her*_____ ___*because she had a little brother, and she was scared*___ ___*that he was going to go on drugs.*___ .

2. "In my neighborhood, it's becoming like that."

   Another student added that _____

   _____

   _____ .

3. "My family knows two people that have had sons or daughters murdered."

   A third student admitted that _____

   _____

   _____ .

4. "There was somebody raped right at the corner of my street."

   Another student reported that _____

   _____

   _____ .

5. "Now that we've grown up with it . . . you get attached to it."

   Heather suggested that _____

   _____

   _____ .

6. "I know that I'm gonna die some way, somehow, so I don't worry about it."

   Kassen declared that _____

   _____

   _____ .

7. "I just don't think that . . . crimes or whatever, will come to me because . . . I just feel like it's not gonna happen to me."

   Koon said that _____

   _____

   _____ .

8 | FOLLOW-UP ACTIVITIES

▨ DISCUSSION QUESTIONS

In groups, discuss your answers to the following questions.

1. What is the best way for schools to maintain safety (metal detectors, uniformed police officers, the principal, parents, student mediators)?

2. In your opinion, is it possible to feel "attached to crime"? Is it possible to feel attached to anything that is terrible because you don't know how to get away from it? Give examples.

▨ ESSAY TOPICS

Choose one of the following topics.

1. In the report, the reporter tells us that the students suggest the same solutions to the crime problem as adults: more parental involvement, fewer guns, and stiffer penalties for crime.

   Do you agree with these suggestions? Which of the three makes the most sense to you? Which of the three makes the least sense? What other suggestions might you make? Write an essay in which you express your opinion.

2. Imagine that you are one of the students at Wakefield High School. Write in your diary about your day. Tell what happened in school. How did you feel about it? What would you like to happen?

▨ SIMULATION: REDUCING CRIME IN THE SCHOOLS

A. Taking Notes to Prepare

*Listen to the report again. Take notes on the issues relating to crime discussed in the report. Key phrases and examples have been provided for you. Use your notes to help you prepare for the follow-up **simulation** on pages 118–122.*

Examples of crime:

weapons taken to school

_____

_____

_____

_____

_____

_____

_____

Teenagers' feelings about crime:

calm acceptance

_____

_____

_____

_____

_____

_____

Attempts to deal with the crime issue:

conflict-resolution programs

_____

_____

_____

_____

_____

B. Simulation

In the report, you heard about the crime teenagers live with every day in an American city. You also heard about the teenagers' feelings about this crime and different ways to deal with crime. Use your notes from the listening and note-taking activity as you prepare your roles for the simulation activity that follows.

For this simulation, the class is divided into four groups: teachers, parents, community leaders, and the school board. Read the situation, choose roles, and after a fifteen-minute preparation, begin the open school board meeting.

THE SITUATION

Arlington's Wakefield High School has just received a grant of $150,000 from the federal government to develop a program to reduce the crime problem in the school and its surrounding neighborhoods.

Teachers, parents, and community leaders have all made proposals to the school suggesting how this money should be spent to begin to solve the crime problem. The school board has reviewed the proposals and will decide how the money should be spent. Before its decision, it will hold an open school board meeting for all concerned to express their opinions. After the meeting, the school board will decide which proposals will be accepted. They will also decide how much money will be allocated to the accepted proposals.

Proposals:

1. Conflict-resolution program

   Rationale:
   If students are educated to take responsibility for their situations and become people who work to solve the problems that lead to crime, they will be less likely to engage in crime themselves.

   Recommendations:
   Require students in the school to spend two hours a week in conflict-resolution and mediation classes. These courses will teach students how to defuse problems before they become bigger. The students will learn how to intervene when they see others fighting.

2. More hiring of social workers

Rationale:
More intervention is needed. Trained social workers should be assigned to work with the students and the families of students who have been involved in crime.

Recommendations:
Hire full-time social workers to work in the schools. They will meet weekly with teenagers who have been involved in crimes or whose families have been involved in crimes. Part-time social workers will visit the families' homes.

3. More security measures

Rationale:
Students will be less likely to bring weapons to school if stronger security measures are taken. There needs to be more supervision at school.

Recommendations:
Introduce more metal detectors at all school entrances. Hire more guards and police officers to patrol the school and its neighborhood.

4. After-school sports programs

Rationale:
If students are more occupied in after-school activities such as sports, they will be less likely to hang out on the streets and become subject to crime.

Recommendations:
More money should be spent on after-school sports activities. Although controversial, one program in particular, "Midnight Basketball," has been shown to be particularly effective in urban areas. Instead of spending the night on the streets, kids are invited to come into the school to play basketball late at night.

(continued on next page)

5. Parental involvement incentives

Rationale:
One of the reasons young people are involved in crime is because their parents are not involved in their lives. If parents were more involved in the school and their children's education, teens would be less involved in crime.

Recommendations:
Set up after-school activities for parents and their children, such as fairs, sports, discussion groups. Encourage parents to volunteer to come to the school once a month as "parent-teacher" to be involved in his or her child's classroom as a teacher's aid. Parents who volunteer their time will be given free training courses in local businesses. These courses could help them get better salaries or find better jobs.

6. Consciousness-raising assemblies

Rationale:
Bringing teachers and students together to discuss the crime problem in an open forum can help raise the students' consciousness about the consequences of crime.

Recommendations:
Offer an honorarium to people (city police officers, reformed criminals, people who have lost a family member to crime) to come to the school to talk about the consequences of crime. Pay teachers overtime salaries to organize and participate in these assemblies.

7. In-service teacher training

Rationale:
Studies have shown that improved classroom instruction has a direct relationship to getting students more involved with their studies and less involved with crime.

Recommendations:
Hire consultants to work with teachers on a long-term basis. Bring in experts who can train teachers to redesign their lessons with an emphasis on whole language and student-centered learning.

THE ROLES

TEACHERS

You teach in Wakefield High School. You are concerned about the quality of education of your students and the safety of the school. Review the proposals to decide which of them would help most to reduce the crime problem at Wakefield High School.

PARENTS

Your children attend Wakefield High School. You are concerned about the fact that weapons have been brought to their school. You are afraid for your children's lives. Review the proposals to decide which of them would help most to reduce the crime problem at Wakefield High School.

COMMUNITY LEADERS

You are a group of religious leaders, businesspeople, and concerned citizens who live in the Wakefield High School neighborhood. If teenagers at Wakefield High are involved in crime, it directly affects you: the safety of the streets, business establishments, and public places. Review the proposals to decide which of them would help most to reduce the crime problem at Wakefield High School.

SCHOOL BOARD

You are a group of elected or appointed community leaders who set school policy. You have reviewed all proposals for reducing the crime problem at Wakefield High School and its surrounding neighborhood. You are interested in hearing the various opinions regarding how the grant money should be spent. You will hold an open board meeting to hear the opinions of all interested people from the community. Then you will make your decision on how to spend the money.

(continued on next page)

THE PROCEDURE

Follow these steps in your simulation.

1. The school board members open the meeting. They invite representatives from each of the three groups (teachers, parents, community leaders) to present their opinions on the proposals.

2. A representative from each group presents recommendations for how to reduce crime in schools.

3. The school board asks questions after each group's presentation. The board can also invite questions from the audience.

4. The school board members vote to decide which proposals will be accepted and how much money will be spent for each one.

5. The school board reports its decision to everyone attending the meeting.

"Attached to Crime" was first broadcast on *Morning Edition*, January 10, 1994. The reporter is Lynn Neary.

MEET YOU ON THE AIR

10

1   PREDICTING

From the title, discuss what you think the interview is about.

2 | THINK AHEAD

In groups, discuss your answers to the following questions.

1. What do you like to do on Saturday nights? Do you think it's important to go out?

2. How do people meet in your country?

3. Some Americans write personal ads to meet people. The following short advertisement is an example of a personal ad:

```
Single, attractive, professional female
seeks handsome professional man (25-30 yrs.)
who likes his work and loves to dance.
```

These people hope that someone will read their ad in a newspaper or magazine and be interested in meeting them. What do you think of this method of meeting people?

3 | VOCABULARY

The following words will help you understand the interview. Try to guess the meaning of the words. Use your knowledge of English, or use your dictionaries. In each set of words, cross out the word that does not have a similar meaning to the highlighted word. Then compare your answers with those of another student. Discuss why these words are similar. The first one has been done for you.

1. **date**	person to go out with	girlfriend/ boyfriend	~~place~~
2. **single**	unmarried	married	alone
3. **chat**	long discussion	small talk	short conversation

4. **match-maker**	person who arranges marriages	go-between	wife
5. **promote**	help	destroy	advertise
6. **banter**	playful talk	joking	argument
7. **sizzling**	cold	burning	passionate
8. **eccentric**	unusual	strange	average
9. **bland**	mild	uninteresting	outrageous

4 | TASK LISTENING

Listen to the interview. You will hear different people talking. As you listen, check the subjects the people talk about.

_____ playing the piano   _____ looking for a job

_____ reading books   _____ eating Chinese food

_____ going to the beach   _____ drinking

5 | LISTENING FOR MAIN IDEAS

Listen to the interview again. The interview has been divided into four parts, each expressing a main idea. You will hear a beep at the end of each part. As you listen, circle the answer that best expresses the main idea in that part. Compare your answers with those of another student.

PART 1   What is *Date Night*?

　　　　a. It's a radio show for singles.

　　　　b. It's a new club for singles.

　　　　c. It's a music show on the radio.

(continued on next page)

PART 2 How did *Date Night* get started?

    a. Susan Block needed information to write a book.

    b. Susan Block wanted to match up people on the air.

    c. Radio listeners asked Susan Block to start it.

PART 3 How would you describe the conversations on the show?

    a. light-hearted conversations

    b. serious conservations

    c. debates about important topics

PART 4 According to Susan Block, why are the personal ads on this show better than personal ads in the paper?

    a. They are edited more carefully.

    b. They are more bland than the personals in the paper.

    c. They give you a sense of the person's personality through their voice.

6   LISTENING FOR DETAILS

Read the questions for Part 1. Then listen to Part 1 again. As you listen, circle the best answer. Compare your answers with those of another student. If you disagree, listen again to Part 1.

PART 1

1. Which of the following is **not** true about *Date Night*?

    a. It's a call-in show.

    b. It's in Los Angeles.

    c. It's a radio station.

2. What do people do after they meet on the air?

   a. They meet in town.

   b. They write to each other's box number.

   c. They become matchmakers.

3. Who is John?

   a. a matchmaker

   b. a famous musician

   c. someone looking for a date

4. Who is Linda?

   a. the host of *Date Night*

   b. a woman who doesn't know what to do

   c. a person whom John wants to talk to

Repeat the same procedure for Parts 2–4.

PART 2

5. What did the show's host do?

   a. She wrote a book on how to play the personals.

   b. She wrote personal ads about herself.

   c. She called people who wrote personal ads.

6. What did Susan Block do on her talk show before *Date Night* started?

   a. She would make up personal ads for individuals.

   b. She expressed her feelings about dating on the air.

   c. She matched up single people who needed each other.

(continued on next page)

PART 3

7. What kind of banter is used on the show?

    a. the same as in a singles' bar

    b. the same as at work

    c. the same as in the movies

8. Which kind of Chinese food is not talked about?

    a. sizzling chicken

    b. hot and sour soup

    c. stuffed dumplings

9. What does the man say you must do when you eat Chinese food?

    a. take off your shoes

    b. share your plates

    c. use chopsticks

PART 4

10. What are personal ads on *Date Night*?

    a. fifteen-word messages

    b. newspaper personals

    c. audio personals

11. According to Susan Block, which are the **best** personals?

    a. the ones with the most information

    b. the ones with nice personalities

    c. the ones with music in the background

12. What does Robert say about himself?

    a. He's thirty-three years old.

    b. He's a passionate eccentric.

    c. He finds women very beautiful.

13. Why doesn't Susan Block like the ads in the paper?

    a. They are too bland.

    b. The information is not true.

    c. The people don't sound attractive.

14. What does she tell people to do when they call in to put ads on her show?

    a. be themselves

    b. be bland

    c. be outrageous

15. What does the woman who calls in say about herself?

    a. She embarrassed somebody she went out with.

    b. She's looking for somebody that's looking for somebody.

    c. Her name is Amy.

7   LOOKING AT LANGUAGE

■ TWO-WORD VERBS

Many verbs are composed of two words in English (verb + preposition). When these two words are combined, they usually have a new meaning.

Exercise 1

Listen to the following sentences from the interview. For each example, focus on the highlighted words. Try to guess the meaning of each two-word verb from the context of the interview. Then write a synonym or definition for each.

1. "I had a wonderful night tonight, I **had** guests **over**, played the piano, had a lot of fun, oh, great."

(continued on next page)

2. "And sometimes what I'd do with a call-in show is, somebody would call in, and—say it was Linda—and I would **make up** a personal for Linda."

_____

3. "And she would express herself and then **get off** the air."

_____

4. "And then maybe Bob would **call in** and say, 'Hey, that Linda, she sounded great, how can I meet her?'"

_____

5. "And I would just feel terrible that I couldn't **match up** poor Bob and poor Linda, who were two single people who needed each other. And I thought, 'I'm gonna do a show like this myself. I'm gonna **match** people **up** on the air,' and that's how _Date Night_ started."

_____

6. "**Tune in** next week; same time, same station, for another Saturday night on _Date Night_."

_____

Now try to match each two-word verb with a synonym or similar expression.

_____ 1. have over

_____ 2. make up

_____ 3. get off (the air)

_____ 4. call in

_____ 5. match up

_____ 6. tune in

a. set the radio or TV to a certain station

b. make a telephone call to a talk show

c. invite to one's home

d. write; create

e. put two people or things together

f. stop talking (on radio or TV)

Exercise 2

Some two-word verbs in English are separable; the verb and preposition can be separated by an object. For example:

*"I'm gonna **match** people **up** on the air."*

In a sentence with a separable two-word verb, the direct object can come between the verb and preposition, or it can come after the verb and preposition:

*"I'm gonna **match up** people."*

However, if a pronoun is the direct object of the sentence, it must come between the verb and preposition; it cannot come after.

*"I'm gonna **match** them **up**."*

Read the following sentences. Each two-word verb is an example of a separable two-word verb. Rewrite the sentences using pronouns as direct objects. The first one has been done for you.

1. Some people don't want to **give up** their freedom just to have a steady boyfriend or girlfriend.

   Some people don't want to give it up just to have a steady boyfriend or girlfriend.

2. In the United States, many people go out in cars. It is common for a man to **pick up** his date at her place.

   _____

   _____

3. People who are engaged to be married sometimes **call off** their engagement just before the wedding.

   _____

   _____

(continued on next page)

4. Some women would like to ask men out for a date, but it's hard for them to pick up the phone and **call up** single men.

_____

_____

5. Some women will go out with a man they've never met before; but it's better to **check out** a man before going on the first date.

_____

_____

8 | FOLLOW-UP ACTIVITIES

■ DISCUSSION QUESTIONS

In groups, discuss your answers to the following questions.

1. Would you call in to the radio show *Date Night* to meet somebody? Why or why not?

2. Susan Block said that some typical questions asked on *Date Night* were: "What kind of work do you do?"; "What movies have you seen?"; and "Do you like Chinese food?" What questions would you ask a person when you first meet? What questions would you *not* ask a person when you first meet?

■ ESSAY TOPICS

Choose one of the following topics.

1. Today people often talk about how difficult it is to meet someone. Do you think that it's more difficult than it was in the past? Why or why not? Write an essay in which you express your opinions.

2. Read the following personal ad, which was presented in the interview:

> Hi. I'm Robert, and I'm forty-three years old, six feet tall, 165 pounds, and I'm in excellent L.A. condition. I'm a passionate eccentric, and I am definitely an acquired taste. Some women have found me very beautiful.

Write your own personal ad for *Date Night*. Mention that part of you that is special.

▨ VALUES CLARIFICATION: DATING

A. Taking Notes to Prepare

By focusing on what people talk about and how they present themselves in the interview, you may have a better background for making judgments in the follow-up **values clarification** on page 134.

Listen to the interview again. Take notes on how the callers looking for a date describe themselves. What categories of information are included in their descriptions? Some examples have been provided for you.

Characteristics of persons looking for a date:

social	_____
musical	_____
_____	_____
_____	_____
_____	_____
_____	_____
_____	_____

B. Values Clarification

Work in groups. Discuss what you look for in a person and why. Read the following criteria that are typically expressed by people who are looking for a date.

Each person in your group should rank these criteria in the order of "most important" (#1) to "least important" (#6). What other criterion would you include? Add it to the list. Compare your ranking with those of others in your group and try to agree on the ranking.

EDUCATION

The person should be well educated. He or she should be intelligent. The person should have gone to good schools and should have a broad understanding of the world.

GOOD LOOKS

The person should be attractive. Dress and appearance are very important.

HUMOR

The person should know how to laugh at life. Being able to joke about things is important.

PERSONALITY

The person should be very social and be able to get along with many different types of people. He or she should like to go to parties and meet new people.

WEALTH

The person should have a lot of money. Money is important in today's world, so it is important to be with someone who can afford to pay for nice things, go on trips, and so on.

OTHER:

"Meet You on the Air" was first broadcast on *All Things Considered*, April 16, 1986. The interviewer is Wendy Kaufman.

THERE ARE WORSE
THINGS THAN DYING

11

PREDICTING

From the title, discuss what you think the interview is about.

2 | THINK AHEAD

Work in groups. Read the following statements. Do you agree with them? See if everyone in your group has the same opinion.

1. Being sick can sometimes be fun.

2. Children cannot accept death and dying as well as adults can.

3. When you are sad, it's best to talk to someone who is the same age as you.

4. When you do not feel happy, it's OK to cry.

3 | VOCABULARY

Read the following sentences. The highlighted words will help you understand the interview. Try to guess the meaning of these words from the context of the sentences. Then write a synonym or your own definition of the words.

1. Smoking is one of the leading causes of ***cancer***. Every year many people die from this disease.

_____

2. When you are sick and don't know what's wrong, it's best to see a doctor. The doctor can usually ***diagnose*** the illness.

_____

3. ***Radiation treatment*** is the most common treatment for cancer patients. It can sometimes stop the disease because the radiation attacks the cancer in the body and destroys it.

_____

4. The bones of the human body are not completely solid; the center of bones is filled with a soft ***bone marrow***.

   _____

5. A ***spinal tap*** is a very painful operation because it removes fluid from the bones.

   _____

6. Dogs and cats usually sleep ***curled up***; they don't lie straight like people do.

   _____

7. People deal with the idea of death and dying differently. Some people feel ***apprehensive*** about death and don't even want to think about it; others are not afraid of death and accept it as a natural part of the life process.

   _____

8. A person who has always lived a healthy and normal life may be ***stunned*** one day to find out that he or she is dying of a disease. People rarely expect this to happen to them.

   _____

9. Some religions teach people that if they are good they will go to ***heaven*** after they die.

   _____

10. Advances in medicine have helped ***cure*** many people of diseases; years ago, these people would have died from the diseases.

    _____

11. Not every treatment will cure a patient of a disease. Even after a long period of feeling well, the patient could experience a ***relapse*** and become sick again.

    _____

(continued on next page)

Now try to match the words with a definition or synonym. Then compare your answers with those of another student. The first one has been done for you.

_f_ 1. cancer	a. identify an illness
___ 2. diagnose	b. suffering from an illness again
___ 3. radiation treatment	
___ 4. bone marrow	c. fearful; scared
___ 5. spinal tap	d. shocked
___ 6. curled up	e. material inside the bones
___ 7. apprehensive	f. a serious disease
___ 8. stunned	g. place some people believe we go to after death
___ 9. heaven	
___ 10. cure	h. make healthy
___ 11. relapse	i. a way to help cancer patients get better
	j. operation to remove fluid from the backbone
	k. putting the body in the form of a ball

4   TASK LISTENING

Listen to the interview. Find the answer to the following question.

Is Jason Gaes cured of cancer?

5   LISTENING FOR MAIN IDEAS

Listen to the interview again. The interview has been divided into four parts, each expressing a main idea. You will hear a beep at the end of each part. As you listen, circle the answer that best expresses the main idea in that part. Compare your answers with those of another student.

PART 1   What's the name of Jason's book?

   a. *A book about kids with cancer*

   b. *A book about my cancer*

   c. *My book for kids with cansur*

PART 2   Why did Jason write the book?

   a. He wanted kids to prepare for his death.

   b. He wanted to write a story with a happy ending.

   c. He wanted to talk about the fun things in having cancer.

PART 3   How does Jason's mother explain his reaction to treatment?

   a. He was afraid of dying.

   b. He wasn't afraid of dying.

   c. He was sure he would never die.

PART 4   How have children reacted to Jason's book?

   a. They have decided to get treatment.

   b. They have felt sick to their stomach.

   c. They have called to talk about their cancer.

6   **LISTENING FOR DETAILS**

Read the questions for Part 1. Then listen to Part 1 again. As you listen, circle the best answer. Compare your answers with those of another student. If you disagree, listen again to Part 1.

PART 1

1. Where does Jason live?

   a. in Omaha, Nebraska

   b. in Washington

   c. in Minnesota

2. How old was he when he was diagnosed with cancer?

   a. eight years old

   b. nine years old

   c. six years old

3. Which of the procedures does Jason describe in his book?

   a. They give you a shot.

   b. They make you move a lot.

   c. They put "Xs" on your head.

Repeat the same procedure for Parts 2–4.

PART 2

4. Who drew the pictures in Jason's book?

   a. his brother Adam

   b. his two brothers

   c. Jason

5. Why didn't Jason like the book *Hang Tough*?

   a. because the boy in the story went through the same things as Jason

   b. because the boy in the story died

   c. because the book wasn't interesting

6. What's fun about having cancer for Jason?

   a. You can have lots of parties.

   b. You get lots of presents.

   c. You can do anything you want to do.

7. Which part of the treatment was the most painful for Jason?

   a. the bone marrow transplant

   b. the spinal tap

   c. the leg pains

PART 3

8. How did Jason want to be treated, according to his mother?

   a. like a sick child

   b. like a needy child

   c. like a normal child

9. Why did Jason say "there are worse things than dying"?

   a. He found out he had cancer.

   b. He didn't want any more painful treatments.

   c. He needed a good ending for his book.

10. How does Jason's mother explain his attitude toward death and dying?

   a. He compares it to being born.

   b. He thinks it's difficult to get to heaven.

   c. He was very afraid of death and dying.

(continued on next page)

PART 4

11. What advice does Jason give to kids?

   a. Don't be scared.

   b. Talk to your mom.

   c. Don't cry.

12. What did Jason tell the little girl who called him?

   a. She would feel a little pain.

   b. She would feel dry and sick.

   c. The operation would work.

13. What last advice does Jason give kids who have cancer?

   a. Never forget that you have cancer.

   b. Try to live a normal life.

   c. Get many treatments.

7 | LOOKING AT LANGUAGE

■ IDIOMS

Several idioms were used in the interview with Jason. Read the following statements as you listen to the tape. Try to determine the meaning of the highlighted idioms in these sentences. Write a synonym or your own definition of each one. Then compare your answers with those of another student.

1. JASON:

   One time I came home with a book, and it was called *Hang Tough*, and I thought *it was really neat* because that boy was going through the same things as I was going through.

   _____

2. JASON:

One time I came home with a book, and it was called *Hang Tough,* and I thought it was really neat because that boy ***was going through*** the same things as I was going through.

---

3. JASON:

And the last two or three pages it told about . . . he died . . . and ***it stunk***.

MONTAIGNE:

It stunk?

JASON:

Uh-huh.

MONTAIGNE:

'Cause he died?

JASON:

Uh-huh.

---

4. MONTAIGNE:

In one page you write that having cancer isn't fun.

JASON:

It ain't no party.

---

5. MONTAIGNE:

Mrs. Gaes, Jason, in his book, writes about some bad moments. ***How did he hold up?***

MRS. GAES:

For the most part, very, very well. Jason insisted on not being treated as a sick child.

(continued on next page)

6. **MONTAIGNE:**

Jason, you wrote this book because you said you were ***tired of*** reading books about kids who had cancer and who died in the end. Was there any time during all this treatment when you thought maybe dying wouldn't be so bad?

_____

7. **JASON:**

When ***it was all over with***.

_____

8. **MONTAIGNE:**

Jason, have kids called you?
JASON:
Yeah, ***you bet!*** Lots of kids have called me.

_____

Now try to match the idioms with another phrase or expression that has similar meaning.

_____ 1. It was really neat!	a. How did he manage?
_____ 2. He was going through something.	b. It was finished.
_____ 3. It stunk.	c. It was terrible.
_____ 4. It ain't no party.	d. It was great!
_____ 5. How did he hold up?	e. Yes, of course.
_____ 6. He was tired of it.	f. It isn't fun.
_____ 7. It was all over with.	g. He was experiencing something.
_____ 8. You bet!	h. He had too much of it.

8   **FOLLOW-UP ACTIVITIES**

▤ DISCUSSION QUESTIONS

In groups, discuss your answers to the following questions.

1. Imagine that Jason Gaes had decided not to continue his treatments. Should a person suffering from a fatal disease be allowed to end his or her life? Should a doctor assist a patient in ending his or her life?

2. Would a book written by a child have more of an effect on another child than a book written by an adult? Why or why not?

▤ ESSAY TOPICS

Choose one of the following topics.

1. Jason said there were worse things than dying. He wasn't afraid of dying because his treatments were so painful. For him, the pain of the treatments was worse than his fear of death.

   How do people in your culture deal with death and dying? Write an essay in which you describe this cultural attitude.

2. Jason wrote a book to help kids with cancer. Have you ever wanted to help people because of something you were going through? Write an essay in which you describe your experience.

▤ ROLE PLAY: DEATH AND DYING

A. Taking Notes to Prepare

*Listen to the interview again. Take notes on Jason's experiences and feelings about having cancer. Key phrases and some examples have been provided for you. Use these notes as background information to help you prepare the follow-up **role play** on pages 146–149.*

(continued on next page)

Jason's feelings about treatment:

radiation is really easy

_____

_____

_____

_____

Jason's feelings about death:

it stinks when someone dies

_____

_____

_____

_____

Jason's advice to cancer patients:

don't wash the Xs off until they're done

_____

_____

_____

_____

B. Role Play

For this role play, the class is divided into four groups. One group will prepare Miriam's arguments. Another group will prepare the arguments of Miriam's sister. Another group will prepare the arguments of Miriam's son. The final group will prepare the arguments of the doctor. Read the situation, choose a group, and after a twenty-minute preparation, begin the discussion.

THE SITUATION

Miriam is sixty-six years old. She has lived alone since her husband died several years ago. Her sister, Emily, lives near her and visits her regularly. Although Miriam does not work, she leads a very active life. She is a member of the local Town Planning Council and is an active member of her church.

Six months ago, however, Miriam was diagnosed as having cancer. She has become very sick over the past few months. The doctor has been treating her with chemotherapy—a treatment that uses chemicals to stop the spread of cancer. The doctors say that she might be cured with this treatment. But there are no guarantees, and many patients experience a relapse of cancer after treatment.

The problem is that the treatment has made Miriam very sick. Each time she goes to the hospital, she becomes very apprehensive because she knows that she will get sick to her stomach. Since she started receiving treatment, she has become very depressed.

This week Miriam made a decision. She decided to stop the chemotherapy. She says that she would prefer to let nature take its course rather than to suffer anymore. Miriam's son, Jack, lives with his own family in another part of the country. When he heard her decision, he became very upset. He decided to go and see his mother; he wants to convince her not to stop the treatment. The doctors have tried to convince her to continue the treatment, too. But Miriam says that she has made her decision. Tomorrow, Miriam's son is coming to see her. Miriam's sister is also coming. They will all discuss Miriam's treatment with the doctor.

(continued on next page)

THE ROLES

MIRIAM

You are very sick from the chemotherapy. It is more painful than you had ever expected. You realize that your life will never be the same with cancer. You have lived a full life. You don't want to continue the treatment. For you, it's worse than dying.

EMILY

You have lived near Miriam for most of your life. You understand Miriam's suffering and feel she should be able to make her own decision about the chemotherapy. Your sister was always very active. You have watched her get more and more depressed. You support her decision to stop the treatment.

JACK

You think your mother is not being rational. You tell her to think of what will happen if she stops the chemotherapy. You believe the treatment can work. You want to convince your mother to continue.

DR. KIRK

You have treated cancer patients for fifteen years. Some of those patients are still living today because of chemotherapy. You realize that Miriam is experiencing a lot of pain, but you want her to understand that chemotherapy is the only way her cancer may be treated.

PROCEDURE FOR DISCUSSION

1. Form new groups to include at least one person playing each of the roles. Miriam, Emily, and Jack meet with Dr. Kirk. Each person presents his or her point of view to Miriam.

2. Miriam listens and reacts to their opinions. Miriam's sister and son try to convince each other of their opinions.

3. After a fifteen- to twenty-minute discussion, Miriam decides what she will do.

4. The group then compares Miriam's decision with the decision of the other groups in class.

"There Are Worse Things Than Dying" was first broadcast on *All Things Considered*, September 16, 1987. The interviewer is Renee Montaigne.

A Healthier Way of Looking at Men and Women

1 PREDICTING

From the title, discuss what you think the interview is about.

2   THINK AHEAD

Work in groups. Read the following statements. Do you agree with them? See if everyone in your group has the same opinion.

1. Both women and men should serve in the military.

2. Women make as good soldiers as men do.

3. Men and women should have different roles in society.

3   VOCABULARY

Read the text. The highlighted words will help you understand the interview. Try to determine the meaning of these words. Then match the words with their definitions or synonyms in the list at the end of the text. Write the number of each word next to its definition or synonym. The first one has been done for you.

Americans have been ***socialized*** to believe that men and women play
different roles. For example, traditionally, male and female roles during
wartime have been clearly defined: Men go to war; they carry the ***burden***
of fighting the war. Women are the ***caretakers***: They stay at home to tend
to family business.

Parents and teachers have reinforced the idea that men usually take
more ***risks***. Men are the independent ones who take chances with the
unknown. In contrast, women are more ***vulnerable***. ***Timid*** as they are
said to be, women must be protected . . . by men.

(continued on next page)

Recently, however, the United States military has begun to change these **_notions_**. New U.S. military policy has presented a different vision of society. According to this new policy, the symbolic G.I. Joe® toy* will now have a female counterpart—G.I. Jane. That is, women and men will both take part in **_combat_**.

But a lot of work will need to be done before society can **_tear down_** the traditional male and female roles. Will society accept that a woman can be a **_bombardier_**, the one who attacks the enemy on foreign land? The new military policy will not be received with **_applause_** by everyone. Will all men become **_pacifists_**, the ones who refuse to fight a war? There will be resistance and maybe even negative **_repercussions_** when women are asked to defend their nation physically along with men.

_____ a soldier who drops bombs from an airplane

_____ a demonstration of approval; clapping hands

_____ shy; easily frightened

_____ people who care for others

_____ ideas

_____ responsibility; duty

_____ easily hurt; sensitive; unprotected

_____ possibilities or chances of meeting danger

_____ fighting; battle

_____ people who believe war should be abolished

_____ indirect and far-reaching effect

_____ destroy; change radically

_1_ educated; taught by society

---

*an American toy, a male military doll

4 │ TASK LISTENING

Listen to the interview. Find the answer to the following question.

How will male and female roles change?

5 │ LISTENING FOR MAIN IDEAS

Listen to the interview again. The interview has been divided into five parts, each expressing a main idea. You will hear a beep at the end of each part. As you listen, circle the answer that best expresses the main idea in that part. Compare your answers with those of another student.

PART 1   According to Berry, how will the new military policy affect men and women?

     a. It will alter the way they see each other.

     b. It will alter the way they see themselves.

     c. both of the above

PART 2   How will the role of women change?

     a. Women will be shot more often.

     b. Women will be defenders of the nation.

     c. Women will see themselves as better than men.

PART 3   What should the concept of a military person be?

     a. A man or woman who kills people for defensive purposes.

     b. A man or woman who relishes a military activity.

     c. A man rather than a woman.

(continued on next page)

PART 4   How will men see themselves?

a. Men will see themselves as people who are supposed to protect women.

b. Men will see themselves as people who can be protected by women.

c. Men will see themselves as people who must take more risks.

PART 5   Will people accept these new roles?

a. They will easily change their minds about male and female roles.

b. They will have a hard time accepting the new roles.

c. They will be unable to adjust to the new roles.

6 LISTENING FOR DETAILS

Read the questions for Part 1. Then listen to Part 1 again. As you listen, circle the best answer. Compare your answers with those of another student. If you disagree, listen again to Part 1.

PART 1

1. What did the defense secretary order the U.S. military to do?

   a. to end its restrictions on women flying combat missions

   b. to restrict women from flying combat missions

   c. to restrict women from serving aboard warships

2. How was this decision received?

   a. with applause from everyone

   b. with applause from Mary Frances Berry

   c. with applause from the U.S. Civil Rights Commission

Repeat the same procedure for Parts 2–5.

PART 2

3. How will the new military policy affect women?

    a. They will be bombed more often.

    b. They will wield more arms.

    c. They will want to be more protected.

4. How might the policy change society?

    a. Women will no longer be caretakers.

    b. New boundaries between men and women will be created.

    c. Our notions of men and women will be enlarged.

PART 3

5. What would cause negative repercussions, according to Berry?

    a. the notion that only women can kill people

    b. the notion that only men can kill people

    c. the notion that people can kill people

6. How does Berry feel about war?

    a. Military activity shouldn't be relished.

    b. War is not such an unpleasant activity.

    c. Not every citizen should share the burden of war.

7. What is healthy for society, according to Berry?

    a. seeing a G.I. Jane doll with a gun

    b. seeing women as pacifists

    c. seeing men as military types

(continued on next page)

PART 4

8. What new role should women play, according to Berry?

   a. people who need protection

   b. people who are aggressive

   c. people who save the lives of men

9. Why does Berry think men will view women differently?

   a. They will understand that women can protect them.

   b. They will be protected by large numbers of women and get used to the idea.

   c. They will think having women around is great.

PART 5

10. Who will have a hard time adjusting to the new roles of men and women?

    a. most men

    b. most women

    c. a lot of military people

11. Why has the old policy been wrong, according to Berry?

    a. It's only practical.

    b. Men, not women, have had to lose their lives.

    c. Women had to take more risks.

7   LOOKING AT LANGUAGE

▨ MODALS

Exercise 1

Read the following statements as you listen to the tape. In each statement, focus on the highlighted modal. Choose the word or phrase that has similar meaning. Circle the correct letter.

1. And that caretakers, therefore—one does not have to assume that caretakers have to be either timid people who have to be protected or that they ***must*** be somehow female.

    a. have to   b. could

2. It ***may*** tear down the boundaries which very much need to be abandoned.

    a. is supposed to   b. could

3. But in a way, it's disturbing to think of women as people who ***can*** kill people.

    a. will   b. are able to

4. It ***could*** have some sort of negative repercussions.

    a. might   b. ought to

5. And no one ***should*** kill other people.

    a. must   b. ought to

6. Not only will American society ***have to*** think about women differently, and, as you said, they will ***have to*** think about men differently.

    a. be obliged to   b. be able to

7. Men will have to view themselves not as people who are ***supposed to*** protect women all the time but as people who can be protected themselves.

    a. required to   b. could

(continued on next page)

8. It just seems optimistic to me to think that men would actually accept the role of being vulnerable, being frightened, and that a woman **might** go out and actually protect him from an enemy attack.

> a. should   b. may

9. If women are going to be in the military—and they are—and they **ought** to have that as an option—they **ought** to take the same risks.

> a. had better   b. should

Exercise 2

Read the following sentences. Decide which modal should be used in each. Think about the ideas expressed in the interview when you make your choice.

1. With the new military policy, men will _____
   (supposed to, have to)
   perceive women and themselves differently.

2. Mary Frances Berry believes that women _____
   (should, might)
   wield arms as men do.

3. Men have traditionally thought of themselves as people who
   _____ protect women.
   (may, are supposed to)

4. The new military policy _____ change male and
   (is supposed to, could)
   female roles in American society.

5. According to Berry, in today's society we _____
   (ought to, can)
   accepte the fact that women, like men, kill people for defensive purposes in wartime.

6. If women protect men in combat, men _____ begin
   (may, have to)
   to accept the traditionally female role of being vulnerable.

7. According to Berry, people's beliefs about male and female roles
   _____ be changed overnight.
   (cannot, ought not to)

8. Berry feels that men _____ not be expected to take
   (may, should)
   more risks than women.

9. It's not true that women _____ be protected.
   (may, must)

10. A lot of people in the military _____ change their
    (will have to, are supposed to)
    perceptions of male and female roles.

8   FOLLOW-UP ACTIVITIES

▩ DISCUSSION QUESTIONS

In groups, discuss your answers to the following questions.

1. Do women serve in the army in your country? In what capacity?
   Would the new U.S. military policy ever be applied in your country?
   Why or why not?

2. Do you agree with Mary Frances Berry that women ought to take the
   same risks as men if they are going to be in the military? Can women
   perform equal roles in the military?

3. Do you agree with Mary Frances Berry's idea that traditionally women
   have been viewed as vulnerable and men have been viewed as
   protective? Is this true in your culture?

▩ ESSAY TOPICS

Choose one of the following topics.

1. Should women, like men, be defenders of their nation? Is this a
   healthier way of looking at men and women? Write an essay in which
   you express your opinion. Use examples from the U.S. military policy
   as described by Mary Frances Berry as well from policies of other
   countries you know.

(continued on next page)

2. Discuss the differences between male and female roles in your country. What roles do *only* men play? What roles do *only* women play? Write an essay in which you compare and contrast male and female roles.

■ DEBATE: SHOULD WOMEN SERVE IN COMBAT?

A. Taking Notes to Prepare

*Listen to the interview again. Take notes on reasons why American women should serve in combat and why they have not served in combat traditionally. One example for each category has been provided for you. Use these notes in the follow-up **debate** on page 161 to help you argue for or against women serving in combat.*

Reasons women have not (traditionally) served in combat:

assumed to be caretakers

_____

_____

_____

_____

Reasons women (like men) should serve in combat:

it will alter the way men and women perceive each other and themselves

_____

_____

_____

B. Debate

For this debate, the class is divided into two teams. The debate will focus on women in combat.

Team A will argue in favor of women serving in combat.

> You believe that women, like men, should serve in combat. They are equal defenders of the nation, and they should share the burden of fighting a war. If women fight in the military, it may help tear down the male/female boundaries that need to be abandoned.

Team B will argue against women serving in combat.

> You believe only men should serve in combat. Men, by nature, are the stronger sex. They should take more risks in their lives than women. One of the key roles of men is to protect women.

Prepare your arguments. Select a moderator to lead the debate.

DEBATE PROCEDURES

Team A begins with a three-minute presentation.
Team B then gives a three-minute presentation.
Team A responds to Team B's presentation for three minutes.
Team B responds to Team A's presentation for three minutes.

After the debate, the moderator evaluates the strength of both arguments.

"A Healthier Way of Looking at Men and Women" was first broadcast on *All Things Considered*, May 1, 1993. The interviewer is Katie Davis.

TAPESCRIPT

IF IT SMELLS LIKE FISH, FORGET IT

Daniel Zwerdling: Now we're going to learn something that every red-blooded American should know—how to shop for fresh fish. If you're a strict vegetarian, listen anyway, and you can pass the information on to your friends. Our classroom is a seafood stall called Pike Place Fish at the Pike Place Market near Seattle's harbor. A lot of customers come here not so much for the food, but for the show. The fishmongers chant every order and toss trout and salmon to each other like footballs. Our teachers are a local chef named Brian Poor and the stall's manager, John Peterson. And, as Poor says, never trust a fish man who looks you deep in the eyes and says, "Of course, all these fish came in just this morning." He says you should inspect the fish yourself following these simple tips.

Brian Poor: What I do is, first of all, go into it and try to see if there is any blood remaining in the backbone area.

Zwerdling: I don't want blood on the backbone?

Poor: You do want blood.

Zwerdling: And, John, why do I want blood inside? It's sort of yucky.

John Peterson: Blood turns brown. If it's got red blood inside of it, it's not old.

Zwerdling: Ah, so red blood means it's—

Poor: You can wash it away, you know. When it turns brown, you can wash it away so people can't see.

Zwerdling: Aha.

Poor: But that's about it.

Zwerdling: OK, so you also say to look at the belly shape. You said this salmon has a nice belly shape. What does that mean?

Poor: Well, like John alluded to, you notice that it looks like he has just been slitted and cleaned. The belly actually looks like it's reattaching itself, as opposed to one that's flat. It has the shape as though it still has the viscera inside.

Zwerdling: Oh, so if it looks a little flattened out— Now, John, you're showing me—

Peterson: That fish is about one-and-a-half days older than the one up here.

Zwerdling: And so we're seeing that the belly is starting to sort of curl in on itself.

Peterson: Actually what it's doing, it's flattening out right up here in the midpart of the belly. It's flattening out instead of still holding its shape, as though, as he said, it still has the viscera in it.

Zwerdling: Now, sometimes I go into a fish store or a fish counter at the supermarket, and I pick up the fish, and it's slimy, and I think, ugh.

Poor: You should go, "Hooray."

Peterson: The melting ice, alone, will remove the slime from the fish. The slime is their clothing. It insulates them when they're in the water so they don't die of exposure. They have to have it.

Zwerdling: So, Brian Poor, the more slime the better.

Poor: The more slime the better.

Zwerdling: OK. What about scales? Sometimes people say—Any clue?

Poor: The more they are handled, the more scales they lose.

Zwerdling: And so this fish right here looks sort of patchy.

Poor: He has been handled more.

Zwerdling: And, John, the fish man, what about eyes? Do eyes give us some sort of clue about fish?

Peterson: If the fish hasn't been iced up they can.

Zwerdling: Somebody told me once, never get a cloudy-eyed fish.

Peterson: Yes and no. I'll show you something on this one right here. That eye is looking real good right there. The eye that's up. The eye that's on the ice is clouded. The ice clouds their eyes.

Zwerdling: Ooooh. But still, it's a real nice fresh fish.

Peterson: Yeah.

Poor: It's a good one. It can be a good one. You can—I have seen fish that were completely spoiled with glassy clear eyes because they had never seen ice; they were in the trunk of a fisherman's car.

Zwerdling: Oh, OK, so eyes are not a great indicator. What about—though—A fisherman once said open the gill, which I'm now doing with my thumb, and make sure it looks nice and bloody inside the gills.

Poor: The Atlantics, these are a farm-raised fish, excellent-quality fish. They'll come in with the gills intact. But typically you won't see gills in gutted fish.

Zwerdling: OK. So if the fish we're looking at has gills in it, we want it to be nice and red and bloody.

Poor: Bloody. Once again, bloody is better.

Zwerdling: Not brown.

Poor: Not brown, not pale—and they pale very quickly in the gill area. This is typically why they are cut out before you get them.

Zwerdling: Brian Poor, do you ever get fish from a supplier? You are at the restaurant, you know, you got a big fish order in, and you go, you sniff, and you think, ugh, these fish are not good.

Poor: What I try to do is I'll stand here and go and I notice no smell here, so I know this is a quality operation because if you go into an environment and you smell fish, then you get out. Because, typically, if the environment smells like fish, the handling of the fish, their practices are not good, don't even bother, move on.

Zwerdling: So if the fish smells like a fish, forget it.

Poor: Exactly, fish—fresh fish—don't smell.

Zwerdling: Tell us your name again?

Peterson: John Peterson.

Zwerdling: Are you the owner?

Peterson: No, I am the manager.

Zwerdling: And it's called—

Peterson: Pike Place Fish.

Zwerdling: And Brian Poor—

Poor: From Chandler's Crab House.

Zwerdling: Thanks a lot.

UNIT 2
LIVING THROUGH DIVORCE

Noah Adams: Betsy, tell me your full name, please.

Betsy Walter: Betsy Allison Walter.

Adams: Betsy Allison Walter, and you're eight years old?

Betsy: Almost nine.

Adams: And you live in Manhattan?

Betsy: Mm-hm.

Adams: And you're in our studio in New York. I appreciate your taking some time to come in and telling us this story. You wrote a letter to the mayor of New York, Mayor Koch.

Betsy: Right.

Adams: Tell me about that, please.

Betsy: Well, I wrote to him because my parents are getting divorced, and I really don't know who to turn to, and I just told him that my parents are getting divorced, and my dad is with somebody else, and I was just getting used to something, and now this, and it's really kinda hard on me, and I'd like an opinion.

Adams: Why did you write to . . . to Mayor Koch?

Betsy: 'Cause he's somebody who I've thought, he's very good to us, I guess, 'cause he's the mayor, and he knows a lot of things, and I thought he would know about this too.

Adams: Yeah. Did you get an answer back?

Betsy: Yes.

Adams: What'd he say?

Betsy: He, um, it's very short. "Thank you for the letter. I was saddened to learn of the difficult times you are experiencing now. It is important for you to share your feelings and thoughts with someone during this time. I wish there is . . . was an easy solution to these problems, but there is not. Please remember that you are loved and that pe— . . . that people care about you. All the best. Sincerely, Edward Koch."

Adams: Mm. Was that reassuring to you, in a way?

Betsy: No.

Adams: No? Did you have any thought in your mind that perhaps he could actually do something about it? For example, call your father, and get your mom and dad back together?

Betsy: No.

Adams: No, you just wanted some advice.

Betsy: But see, I tried to sometimes, like, 'cause I had a dance recital one day, and I'd invite 'em both, but I wanted them to sit next to each other, but they didn't.

Adams: Yeah. What other advice have you been able to come across? To . . . to find?

Betsy: Well, the guidance counselor, she said that it . . . a lot of kids have the same problems; say, there're 400 in school, say, and like 300 of them have the same problem.

Adams: Sure—sure. You know, most people you talk with will have had parents who were divorced.

Betsy: Oh.

Adams: Yeah. Most people. It's kind of a sad thing, but most people get through it all right, too. That's my advice for you.

Betsy: Thank you.

Adams: You wrote another letter to somebody who, who had written a book called *The Boys' and Girls' Book of Divorce*?

Betsy: Yes.

Adams: A psychologist?

Betsy: Mm-hm.

Adams: And what did that person tell you?

Betsy: Well, he said that I should try another of his books to find out help.

Adams: Oh, he wanted you to go out and buy his book. Did you?

Betsy: Well, we had the one he recommended.

Adams: And how did that go? What did you think of that one?

Betsy: Well, the problem is, he puts things in a way that I can't really quite get it through me, that I already know, and I want some, really, advice that my questions really are—not just answers that people keep telling me over and over again.

Adams: Can you give me an example, Betsy?

Betsy: Why did they get divorced? What happened?

Adams: Do you think that . . . that parents sometimes don't think children are old enough to understand or can't handle it, and so will hide some information?

Betsy: Yes.

Adams: Not that they have to say everything, but you think there ought to be a little bit more sharing of the information.

Betsy: Yeah, my . . . that's what my mom said.

Adams: Yeah. And in terms of their own divorce, do you understand it better now?

Betsy: No.

Adams: No? Why? What still don't you understand about that?

Betsy: Well, why did they have to go off and do it, 'n' 'cause, see, the most painful part is when I saw my dad packing up, and, and I really don't understand because, like, it's hard to, 'cause they won't tell me what happened to them, and I really want 'em back together and I don't understand why they can't.

Adams: Yeah. What do you think you've learned from this, do you think if . . . if somebody else in school, for example, told you that their parents were getting divorced, how do . . . how do you think you could advise them?

Betsy: Well, I wrote a book, and I said, and I think I would say the same information that I said.

Adams: You wrote a very small book?

Betsy: Yeah.

Adams: Yeah. Do you have it there?

Betsy: Mm-hm.

Adams: Could you read some of it for me, please?

Betsy: All right. Let me get it. It's called *A Book About Divorce*. Should I read the whole book, it's short?

Adams: Sure.

Betsy: "It's not your fault when your parents get divorced. Why does it have to be you? Because Mommy and Daddy don't love each other any more. Remember: it's OK to be sad and cry. Tell someone about your feelings." That's it.

Adams: That's nice. Listen, Betsy, thank you for talking with us. I appreciate it, and I . . . and I wish the best. I hope things go well for you.

Betsy: Thank you.

Adams: And maybe, maybe this is the beginning of a writing experience for you, and you can grow up to be a writer.

Betsy: I don't want to. But I want to write like one book that would make it, but not a whole series, you know.

Adams: You just want to write a book and make a lot of money.

Betsy: No, not money, just famous.

Adams: OK. OK, Betsy, thank you. Good night.

Betsy: OK, good night.

UNIT 3
A COUCH POTATO

Susan Stamberg: Robert Armstrong, a cartoonist and illustrator in Dixon, California, claims to have coined the phrase "couch potato" back in 1976. The phrase just doesn't seem that old, although the tradition of lounging on a couch, surrounded by junk food and fizzy drinks, eyes fixed on the TV set, that tradition is certainly time honored. In addition to the phrase, Mr. Armstrong is founder and head of Couch Potato Clubs around the country. There are 8,500 members, he says. They get an official Couch Potato handbook, plus newsletters and the obligatory T-shirt. Robert Armstrong says this is an important weekend for Couch Potatoes.

Robert Armstrong: The holidays are always important; it's a family time; everyone watches the football games; at least the menfolk are in there watching the football game, and the women are in some other room, maybe the kitchen, 'er talking about family matters, or other matters, and . . . uh . . . in some respects, it's one way for all these different people in the family to get . . . they . . . to get together in one room and tolerate one another, around the video hearth, that is, watching TV.

Stamberg: So it helps keep the peace over a long family weekend, huh?

Armstrong: Yeah, if they have nothing else in common, they can all watch the same TV program. And there's a definite need for a group like the Couch Potatoes, I think.

Stamberg: What do you think the need is?

Armstrong: I think, firstly, there are a lot of people that suffer from intellectual guilt about how much TV they watch, and . . . uh . . . for years it's been everyone's little dirty secret about TV watching—and how much they watched—and people would lie about it, and we as Couch Potatoes beckon people to "come out of the closet," and claim it loud that they are a "tuber and proud." The "tuber" part of it is one of the reasons why we selected the potato to be our icon, because it is, after all, a tuber, and has many eyes.

Stamberg: Oh, I just got it—as in tube!

Armstrong: Yes, watching the tube, and all the eyes of the potato used to watch TV with. It just, seemed like a . . . a good symbol for us to rally around. And . . . uh . . . though, I think many outsiders have . . . uh . . . teased us about our physiques taking on a sort of a potato shape after awhile, but . . . uh . . . that's not necessarily bad; have a potato shape, it gives you the needed ballast so you don't roll off the couch quite so readily.

Stamberg: *(laughing)* What's usually highest on the Couch Potatoes' hit parade of TV shows—would it be *Love Boat*?

Armstrong: That's just one that came to mind, but we have so many members, from such a wide cross-section of walks of life, that . . . uh . . . I'd have to say that any show would be a recommended Couch Potato show. In fact, we have a slogan we live by, "If it's on TV, it must be good."

Stamberg: Words to live by, for all you Couch Potatoes out there. Robert Armstrong in Dixon, California. A man of very discriminating taste, obviously. He is the founder and head of Couch Potato Clubs around the nation, a position, I'm sure, cheers his mother.

UNIT 4
THE BIBLE HOSPITAL

Linda Wertheimer: Patience is a virtue for Patrick Kirby, who owns the Bible Hospital in Alexandria, Virginia. He's a restorer of books and he does much of the work by hand. He restores books mostly for libraries, but about 20 percent of his work is rebinding private books, mainly bibles. His shop has rolls of imitation leather for the covers, gold and silver foil for stamping titles and names, tubs of glue, and a huge paper cutter.

Most of the bibles he restores are small ones, meant to be carried to church. He says he only gets about fifteen of the large leather-bound family bibles per year.

Patrick Kirby: This one has to be resewed, completely resewed.

Wertheimer: So you'll have to put the pages back together.

Kirby: Right.

Wertheimer: By the way, it's fallen apart. Well now, in that place where it's all worn off, where the tooled-leather cover and the spine are split and it's—there's this piece of worn-looking leather, how—what are you going to do?

Kirby: It'll be a new piece of leather. This piece of leather here will be lifted off the board here, pulled back about an inch or so, then we'll reinsert a new piece of leather in here. We'll glue that back down and then we'll take the spine and paste that over the new spine.

Wertheimer: What about these little hand bibles? Bibles are inexpensive. You can get them everywhere.

Kirby: Oh, yeah, yeah.

Wertheimer: Why do people want to—

Kirby: Sentimental.

Wertheimer: Yeah?

Kirby: Sentimental value.

Wertheimer: Do they tell you about them when they bring them in to you so you'll know how to—

Kirby: Yeah, you can look in them and see the date it was—date given—that somebody gave it to them. That it was given to them when they were baptized or confirmation or something like that. Yeah.

Wertheimer: What are the books that individuals bring in to you besides the Bible? What is the precious book that comes in here?

Kirby: The cookbook.

Wertheimer: The cookbook?

Kirby: Oh, yeah!

Wertheimer: Well this one, which is sitting right in front of me, is a '60s edition of *The Joy of Cooking*. I guess, of course, cookbooks are in dangerous places. Kitchens.

Kirby: Yeah, they bring them in and I say to them, "Well, you might be able to buy a—get a new cookbook for cheaper than what you'll pay to have this done." And they'll say, "They just don't have the information in the new ones like they do—the old ones." Plus, they have all their little notes and everything in them.

Wertheimer: And all the little stains, I see in this cookbook. They have little checks by this—whoever owns this cookbook has made checks by recipes that they like or tips that they think are important. And there's a nice spot right on "Cheese Nut and Bread Loaf." How long have you been doing this?

Kirby: Well, my dad, he passed away in '69, and I took over then.

Wertheimer: So, how long has the Kirby family been in the bookbinding business?

Kirby: He started in 1939, and he did everything by hand, I mean, he didn't—today I have a few machines here that he didn't have.

Wertheimer: But it looks to me like a lot of this equipment is at least as old as you are.

Kirby: Yes. I know that the stamper and the cutter and the little vise backer here, they're older than I am.

Wertheimer: And did they all come from your dad's shop?

Kirby: Yeah.

Wertheimer: So, you still do a lot of the things in the old way, as well.

Kirby: Yes, except for sewing a book, we use a machine is all.

Wertheimer: And he did it by hand?

Kirby: Hand, yeah. Hand sewing would take about an hour, whereas if you sewed it on a machine it would take about less than five minutes, plus it probably does a better job too.

Wertheimer: So, are you going to pass this on to the next Kirby in line?

Kirby: My children aren't really interested in this business. I guess once I'm gone, I don't know what'll happen. Maybe I'll just sell the business someday and retire.

Wertheimer: Patrick Kirby of the Bible Hospital. It's *All Things Considered*.

UNIT 5
A BOY'S SHELTER FOR STREET PEOPLE

Lynn Neary: It was about two years ago, on a cold night in December, when eleven-year-old Trevor Ferrell first realized that there were people living out on the streets of Philadelphia, just twelve miles from his nice, comfortable suburban home. Trevor saw a news report about the city's homeless. He ran to tell his parents about this startling discovery. Trevor wanted to do something, right away, that night. He wanted his mother and father to take him into the city so he could help someone. His amazed parents resisted the idea at first, but then relented, thinking it would be a good lesson for their impressionable son. They never expected he would want to do it again. They didn't realize what else Trevor would learn that night.

Trevor: I saw a man living on the street, when we got into the city, and I brought in a blanket and a pillow that night, and I gave it to the man, and he looked really comfortable, and said "God bless you," and it made me feel really good.

Neary: It felt so good that Trevor went back the next night, and the next, and the next. Pretty soon, his family ran out of pillows and blankets and old clothes. So they put an ad in a local paper for donations. The paper decided to find out what Trevor and his family were up to, so they interviewed him, and his story was published. Donations poured in; people volunteered to help; someone contributed a van. So they started giving out free food as well, and now, there is a permanent shelter for the homeless in Philadelphia, dubbed Trevor's Place by the people who stay there. Trevor's story is the subject of a book, *Trevor's Place*, written by his parents, Frank and Janet Ferrell. Trevor's initial act of kindness has become a full-time commitment, and Trevor has become close friends with many of the people he met on the streets.

Trevor: There's Chico, Ralph, um . . . Big Joe . . . there's a lot.

Neary: Well, who are the street people? What's their background? How did they get to be living in the street?

Trevor: Well, some of them lost their jobs, some of them, um, have mental problems, some of them drink, and all it takes is for yuh, for somebody to be out in the streets for two or three days, and then you start looking dirty, and it's . . . it's really hard. My Dad and I tried staying on the street one night, and we couldn't even try—we couldn't take it; we had to leave.

Neary: How . . . how long did you . . . how long did you try it, Frank?

Frank Ferrell: Oh, for about three or four hours, and then we gave up. Uh, we had a home to go back to, and . . . uh . . . we had the shelter of our car . . . uh, but, uh . . . and you'd think we would have been able to. I'm not too proud of that, are you, Trev, that we couldn't do it? Uh, . . . the, the . . . the streets are cold, filthy, uh, how cold was it, Trevor, it was about thirty . . .

Trevor: Not that cold!

Ferrell: No, it was about thirty-eight degrees or something, and I thought, "well, that's not going to be so bad." Well, it *was* so bad, and we had sleeping bags with us, and we thought, uh, we'd be able to stand it. But, uh, the sidewalk's awfully hard, uh, you see raw sewage here and there, it's, it's not easy. And those people, uh, that spend their lives out there, uh, I don't know how they do it.

Neary: And yet you go down there frequently, all the time. At one point, I think you were going every night.

Ferrell: Yes, uh, the vans now, there, it's a big operation. The vans go in every night, uh, serving homeless people food—food that's, uh, generously donated by fast-food chains, and, uh, there are volunteer . . . uh . . . coordinators of the effort, uh, individual families. There are over a hundred families in the Philadelphia area that cook on a regular basis, and food is . . . is . . . taken in and given freely, unconditionally to people that . . . that are on the streets and obviously have a need for, uh, for someone, so much more of a need for the . . . the caring that's exchanged than really the . . . the food, I guess.

Neary: What kind of reaction do you get from the street people when . . . when you go down there and . . . and start giving things away? 'N' it . . . was it different when you began? Has it changed over the course of time, or, do you get a variety of reactions?

Trevor: We get a lot of different reactions, a lot of them—they're all good, though. Like, they all accept the food, 'n' nice; some of them might not accept the food, but after a while, we'll wear them down, and they'll accept the food.

Neary: What do you mean "wear them down"?

Trevor: Like, they'll say no, but every night, we'd ask them, 'n' they'd say OK.

Ferrell: Yeah. Eventually, eventually, they say yeah, uh, and initially they, most of them say yes, uh, because it's a youngster that's offering it to them, and not someone towering over them and looking down on them, and saying "What are you doing out here, you ought to get a job?" Uh, kids are non—they're not judgmental, and uh, they're not threatening; they're just doing it, because of a heartfelt need to, want to reach out to somebody.

Neary: Trevor, this must have . . . this must have changed your life completely.

Trevor: Yeah, well I'm not allowed to . . . I'm not . . . I'm allowed, but I'm not able to play with my friends as much, and have as much fun as I used to. But it's all worth it: helping the homeless people on the streets, and seeing how grateful they are.

Neary: Mm-hm. Well, how has it changed you?

Trevor: Well, I know that . . . I've learned that people may look scary, but they're really nice, and to treat people not just because of what they look like or anything.

Neary: So you were scared when you first went down there.

Trevor: The first night, yes, but now I know there's nothing to be afraid of.

Neary: Trevor Ferrell and his father Frank Ferrell, who along with Trevor's mother, Janet, and with the help of Edward Waken, has written a book about his son's campaign for the homeless, called *Trevor's Place.* Proceeds from the book are being donated to Trevor's campaign.

UNIT 6
THE FOUR NEW FOOD GROUPS

Renee Montaigne: Our parents said it; so did our teachers in health class: To grow up big and strong and to stay healthy, you needed to eat something each day from each of the four basic food groups—meat, fruits and vegetables, dairy products, and bread and cereal. For thirty-five years, the food groups remained unchallenged—that is, until the Physicians Committee for Responsible Medicine stepped in. Dr. Neal Barnard is president of the organization, and he joins us now in our studio. Good morning.

Dr. Neal Barnard: Good morning.

Montaigne: You're recommending four new food groups to replace the ones that we all grew up with. What are they?

Barnard: The new four food groups are grains, legumes—meaning beans and related foods—vegetables, and fruits. And as a group, there is no cholesterol in the new four food groups, and they're very high in fiber.

Montaigne: Now, grains—I always think of bread and cereal, but . . .

Barnard: It's—it's really more than that. It's not only the breads and the cereals and oatmeal, it's also—pasta; spaghetti and linguini are all in the grain group. It's rice —all the grains. The legume group is beans and lentils and peas—anything in a pod. And what we've found is that groups that—population groups that center their diet on these new four food groups live years longer and have much healthier lives.

Montaigne: You've left out some dairy products. Why?

Barnard: Really, for a couple of reasons. First is: People have the hope that if they consume dairy products, they'll have strong bones. Well, for years researchers have measured the bone density of postmenopausal women who are developing osteoporosis, and they found that dairy products just don't work if the goal is to prevent osteoporosis. It just doesn't work. And it turns out that what's more important is actually moderating one's protein intake. In other words, if we're on a high-meat diet, the large amount of protein that people are eating actually leeches calcium out of the bones, and it's lost in the urine. If you reduce your protein intake, the calcium stays in the bones and that's what seems to be more important in maintaining strong bones. The milk just wasn't doing the job at all.

Montaigne: Why did you leave meat entirely off the list? It's now an option. After—I mean, after all, consumers are more aware than ever of the potential problem of fat in their diets and producers offer leaner cuts of meat.

Barnard: Well, none of them are truly lean. Even the new McLean burger that McDonald's has been pushing—that burger is 49 percent fat. You just can't have meat that is anywhere near the low-fat content of the legumes and the grains and the vegetables and so forth. And the reasons, medically, are profound. It's not just the 4,000 heart attacks every day; it's not just the fact that people are fatter than they want to be; it's also other illnesses—breast cancer, for example.

When I was a medical student, we had no idea that breast cancer was related to foods that people put on their plate. All we were taught was mammograms. Well, when I was in medical school, breast cancer claimed one in eleven women. And when I was a resident, it was one in ten. Now it's one in nine. But it was ten years ago that the National Research Council issued a report showing that dietary factors lead to breast cancer—principally, the large amount of fat that's in the meat and the dairy products. So we decided, let's—let's get them off the four food groups. People don't need to eat them. If they skip them, they'll be healthier.

Montaigne: The American Farm Bureau—Federation—obviously, is opposed to your proposals. So is a former agriculture secretary, John Clark. Do you really think—and just very briefly—the U.S. Department of Agriculture will set these new—will adopt your recommendations?

Barnard: It will take time for the Department of Agriculture to change, but medically, we've got no choice. The medical leaders are now united in the fact that we've got to change and change dramatically, and change particularly for our children.

Montaigne: Thank you very much. Dr. Neal Barnard is president of the Physicians Committee for Responsible Medicine, a nonprofit advocacy group based here in Washington, D.C.

UNIT 7
THE DIRTY DOZEN

Emil Guillermo: If you're at the beach for this Memorial Day weekend, take a look in the surf. Notice anything? A cigarette butt perhaps, maybe some plastic or a kitchen sink. One day last year, volunteers spent three hours combing the coasts of the United States, Canada, Mexico, Guatemala, and Japan. They picked up more than 1,200 tons of trash, most of it plastic. Patty Devonham wrote the annual beach cleanup report for the Center for Marine Conservation and she joins us now to discuss it.

Now three years ago, we read a lot about medical waste washing up along the Eastern seaboard; yet your report says it's—it's actually a very small portion, less than one-tenth of 1 percent of the debris found along the coasts, so that appears not to be the big problem. So what is?

Patty Devonham: The big problem is the everyday items that any one of us can contribute to the ocean. The dirty dozen, which is the top twelve items that we find on the beach, are things like Styrofoam cups, plastic eating utensils, plastic beverage bottles—a lot of things that could be recycled. Metal cans, glass bottles—those things are the most prevalent items on the beach and they don't need to be there.

Guillermo: But primarily plastics.

Devonham: Sixty-four percent of all the trash was plastic.

Guillermo: Well, a lot of people think of plastic as—as harmless, as inert, a nuisance more than anything else. How—how does it threaten marine life?

Devonham: First of all, we really are concerned about the problems to animals. They can either get tangled up in plastic items or eat it. When they eat it, sometimes the concept is that they feel that they're full so they stop eating and they starve; or it will block their digestive tract and when they get tangled, it doesn't grow—or give any more and they can either be—get wounds and constricted or strangulation. Thirty thousand northern fur seals die each year because of entanglement, and that is one of the few studies that we've been able to undertake.

Guillermo: Now who's responsible for dumping all of this stuff, I mean I—I imagine there—there can be some links, but it—how hard or how easy is it to tell who's responsible?

Devonham: Well, it's very difficult. Those top twelve items I identified, anybody can dump. But there are groups that we are able to tell directly are responsible for dumping trash illegally into the ocean. For example, one group that's very easy is the cruise ships—they write their name on everything.

Guillermo: So is there any kind of aggressive effort to go after these industries?

Devonham: There is a law. The Coast Guard is responsible for enforcing the Marpol Annex Five treaty, which says you can't dump plastics anywhere. It talks about other trash items as well. The Coast Guard has a lot to do. They need more resources and they also need to make sure that this is a top priority and they are investigating and they are enforcing fines, but we want it to be even more active and we want people to understand the implications to wildlife and to the environment.

Guillermo: But if there's all this trash coming up on the beaches, it—it—it indicates that they don't really take it seriously, do they?

Devonham: You're right. A lot of people don't think of a litter problem as serious, but this is beyond that. This is costing millions of dollars to clean up every year. Communities want to make sure people come back to their tourist area, their beach area, so they clean it up and they spend, for example, in Santa Monica, California, $1.3 million just to clean up a quarter-mile stretch of beach.

Guillermo: Patty, thank you very much. Patty Devonham manages the marine debris program at the Center for Marine Conservation here in Washington.

UNIT 8:
FROM ONE WORLD TO ANOTHER

Roberta Hill Whiteman: *I'uni Kwi Athi? Hiatho.*
White horses, tails high, rise from the
   cedar.
Smoke brings the fat crickets,
trembling breeze.
Find that holy place, a promise.
Embers glow like moon air.

Susan Stamberg: Roberta Hill Whiteman, reading from her first published collection of poetry, *Star Quilt.*

Whiteman: Will you brush my ear? An ice bear
   sometimes lumbers west.
Your life still gleams, the edge melting.
I never let you know.
You showed me how under snow and
   darkness,
grasses breathe for miles.

Stamberg: Roberta Hill Whiteman dedicated this poem to her father, using his Oneida Indian name for the title.

Whiteman: My father was Oneida and Mohawk. He raised us. My mother died when I was very young and . . . um . . . I never really thanked him. He died in the late sixties, when I was in my early twenties, and so, this poem, in a way, is trying to thank him for raising me.

Stamberg: Where did you grow up?

Whiteman: I grew up in Green Bay, Wisconsin, which is about ten miles from the Oneida reservation.

Stamberg: Not on the reservation itself.

Whiteman: No, I didn't grow up on the reservation. Uh . . . and a lot of times, we would go out there, but it's a very small reservation, and I did not grow up on it.

Stamberg: Mm-hm.

Whiteman: It's about eight by ten miles.

Stamberg: And do you feel, uh . . . uh . . . in going back, in . . . in going from Green Bay to Oneida, that you are moving from one world to another?

Whiteman: Oh, yes! Oh, yes! I find there is quite a difference. When I go to Oneida . . . um . . . there's just this real feeling of uh . . . of everything being connected to each other, to the people, to the land, to the . . . the long-ago. That there is a sense of uh . . . of community, and I never really felt that as a child. Um . . . as a child, I often felt that I was somehow exiled . . . uh . . . that I ended up in this very large place, and that . . . that I didn't quite understand or I didn't feel connected to the other people around me.

Stamberg: Mm-hm.

Whiteman: And I think in . . . in one way that's why I turned to poetry. It made me feel connected to things.

Stamberg: Hah; hah. Because I wanted to ask you, what influences your poetry most, do you think? The fact that you are Indian, or the fact that you are a woman, or the fact that you are a wife, or a mother, or a daughter? Because you write about all of those things.

Whiteman: Well, I think, as a child, my grandmother was a Mohawk, and she used to tell us a . . . lots of stories, and she loved poetry, and as a child, some of the books that we had were her books of poetry, and I often spent a lot of time . . . uh . . . poring over her books or listening to her talk. And I think I found in language . . . um . . . pictures in my mind that made me feel really happy or helped me to deal with things. And um . . . I don't think it's any one particular part of my uh . . . social being, mother, or . . . or whatever, my . . . my heritage, but I think it is that that voice that my grandmother made me pay attention to.

Overcast Dawn
This morning I feel dreams dying.
One trace is this feather
fallen from a gull,
with its broken shaft,
slight white down,
and long dark tip
that won't hold air.
How will you reach me
if all our dreams are dead?

Stamberg: You write a lot about natural things, and . . . and deal with nature in . . . in ways that I've not come across before. I wonder if that 's where . . . um . . . maybe that Indian heritage really . . . uh . . . shows through, just being able to look at a feather that way.

Whiteman: My father . . . uh . . . tried to get me to listen and to pay attention, and . . . uh . . . I guess that's where part of that comes from.

Stamberg: Roberta Hill Whiteman, her first collection of poetry is called *Star Quilt*. It's published by the Holy Cow Press in Minneapolis. It has a forward by the poet Carolyn Forché.

UNIT 9:
ATTACHED TO CRIME

Bob Edwards: Only a few years ago, schoolchildren packed lunch boxes, and now more and more of them are packing weapons. We read about it every day. "Crisis of violence, a menace to childhood," says the *Washington Post.* "Violence hits one in four students," reports the *New York Times,* and *Newsweek* declared that "Our children are growing up scared." Surely some communities have escaped the trend, but too many have not. NPR's Lynn Neary visited a high school in Virginia and has this report.

Lynn Neary: Arlington's Wakefield High School is not necessarily a typical American public school. It is probably more diverse, both ethnically and economically, than most schools. Thirty-six percent of the school is Hispanic, 15 percent Asian, 24 percent black, and 23 percent white. Many of the students would describe themselves as middle class or working class. Many are poor. It is a suburban school, set in a neighborhood of small, attractive, single-family homes. But Washington, D.C., is just a short drive away.

We sat down the other day with a small group of Wakefield students. These are responsible and committed kids who take part in the school's conflict-resolution programs. They have been trained as mediators who can step into a dispute and help defuse it before it gets out of control. The school principal asked us to use only first names, and we agreed. All the students, with one exception, had concrete examples of how crime has affected their lives.

Wakefield Student: It does affect me because I have a little brother and I'm scared that he's getting on drugs or something, because of his friends.

2nd Wakefield Student: It affect me hearing about guys shooting each other, and, like, in my neighborhood, it's becoming like that, that kind of stuff now, guys walking around with knives, making up gangs and stuff like that.

3rd Wakefield Student: I live in a nice, relatively nice, neighborhood, but, still, my family knows two people that have been—that have had sons or daughters murdered, and there's one whose son was convicted of murder.

4th Wakefield Student: Not too long ago, around where I live, there were two people murdered, and then there was someone who lived next door to me, they were, you know, involved in a drive-by. So, I mean, when I see that, and you know, I'm thinking, this is my neighborhood, I mean, I could easily have been on that street.

5th Wakefield Student: Well, there was somebody raped right at the corner of my street. There was a girl raped not too far, a couple blocks away, and so I personally feel like, OK, I can walk outside, but my family's really against it.

6th Wakefield Student: See, I live in a valley, so— It's Green Valley, it's like one of the worst places to live, and I lived there for like six years and nothing had happened to my family personally—Well, once to my mom, she got robbed, but that's because you have to expect it there.

Neary: For someone of another generation, that calm acceptance of crime as a fact of life was chilling. It was a theme heard over and over again.

7th Wakefield Student: You see stuff on the news where, like, you know, big, you know, humungous racial-type tension things, you know, and I mean, you think, you know, "Wow, that's really bad," but, I mean, there's other things that are considered a norm.

Neary: Chad is an eighteen-year-old senior.

Chad: It's, like, when I go to a party. I mean, almost all the time, there's some kind of fight that starts out. So, I mean, it's sort of like, you know, something that involves a, you know, a weapon or something. So, I mean, a lot of it's got to be a norm, you know, a normal type thing.

Neary: A weapon as in, you go to a party and almost always somebody, what, pulls a knife or a gun?

Chad: Somebody—yeah. Somebody pulls a knife, pulls a gun. I mean, they're just—they're either, like, you know, they're drunk or they're, you know, just, I mean, they're just not thinking, so I mean, I almost, you know, I sort of expect it to happen.

Neary: What happens at a party when someone pulls out a gun?

Chad: Most of the time everybody runs.

Neary: Weapons at parties and on the street may be commonplace, but what about at school? Wakefield, these kids insist, is less violent now than it was a few years ago. A strong security program is partly responsible for the improvement. The kids know that, but they also resent some of the security measures. Still, they say they feel safe at Wakefield, and they're glad the school has not installed metal detectors. But they know that banned items, like beepers and some weapons, are in the school. Kassen is a nineteen-year-old senior.

Kassen: I still even see another guy back me up in the bathroom and put a knife up my throat. I said, "Hey, man, I'm not paying, all right?" And then he leaves me, but I don't let things like that bother me because I don't carry any weapons or anything because I don't need it.

Neary: A lot of kids, these students say, are not able to protect themselves, so they seek safety in numbers. And that, says sixteen-year-old Koon, is why there are a lot of gangs.

Koon: Everybody feel like I'm in danger because of that gang, so they join gangs, and there's another gang, you know? And it all builds up. But, it all started out with maybe a couple of people who just feel like, "Oh, let's dress alike, it's cool that way," you know? And then all of a sudden they go, "Oh, let's develop a name," and then they develop a name. "Oh, let's get some more people," and then more people will join. And then they go, "Oh, let's have certain rules to go by," you know, like the Boy Scouts or whatever. And then they go by certain rules and if you can't follow that, you can't be in that group. And then it goes on like that.

Neary: The solutions, these kids suggest, are the same ones you hear from adults—more parental involvement, fewer guns, stiffer penalties for crime. But the kids don't hold out much hope that anything is going to change soon. The reality of crime, says eighteen-year-old Heather, will be inextricably entwined with their memories of youth.

Heather: Now that we've grown up with it, it's just like growing up in a neighborhood. You attach—you get attached to it. We're attached to crime. I mean, we—you can't get away from it, so what do you do? You can't—you can't run. And a lot of people, you can't run; they join them. I mean, that's basically how it is.

Neary: Some do want to run. Kassen, who feels pressured by the gangs in his neighborhood, wishes he could move.

Kassen: I do because my neighborhood is getting worse every day. I would rather live out in the country, you know, where there's less people and less gangs and stuff like that. I think it would be better.

Neary: Do you ever worry that you're going to get killed, Kassen?

Kassen: I know that I'm gonna die some way, somehow, so I don't worry about it. No, just—sometimes I do think about it, you know? Just got to leave it where you have.

Neary: But others say you can't escape it. There is no place where you can get away from crime completely, so there is that acceptance. More than acceptance, really, an insistence that crime will not stop them from living their lives. And sixteen-year-old Koon, who says she lives in the worst neighborhood in the area, is probably the most defiant.

Koon: I just don't think that it'll come to me, crimes or whatever, will come to me because, I don't know, I just feel like it's not gonna happen to me.

Neary: It's really interesting to hear what you're saying because you're saying, "It doesn't affect me, but—"

Koon: I don't let it affect me.

Neary: —it's all around you, I guess is what you're saying at the same time.

Koon: Yeah. I don't let it affect me because if I let—if I keep sitting home and worry about it, then I'll probably sit home the whole rest of my life and not go out of my house.

Neary: At one point during our discussion, we could hear a walkie-talkie in the hall. It was the security guards checking up on some suspicious-looking kids hanging out near the school, but nothing ever came of it and no one gave it a second thought. It was just a routine event in a school with a student body that probably can't imagine a time when school felt safe without security guards.

UNIT 10:
MEET YOU ON THE AIR

Susan Block: It's not just another Saturday night. It is Susan Block's *Date Night,* and I'm Susan Block!

Wendy Kaufman: A call-in show for singles. Every Saturday night, on Los Angeles radio station KIEV. People meet on the air; they chat, and if they want, they write to each other's box number. Susan Block plays matchmaker.

Susan: Let's get personal with John. Hi there, John.

John: Yeah, hello, how are you?

Susan: I'm just fine, how are you?

John: Oh, fine. I had a wonderful night tonight, I had guests over, played the piano, had a lot of fun, oh, great.

Susan: I hear the piano.

John: Oh, yeah, it's me. *(sings)*
More than the greatest love the world has known.
This is the love I'll give to Linda alone.

Susan: Linda! Linda, where are you? C.J., get Linda on the line. She'll have to . . . she'll have to hear how she's being serenaded to. . . .

John: Serenaded, yeah!

Susan: OK, Linda?

Linda: Yes?

Susan: How did you like that serenade?

Linda: Oh, that was very nice.

Susan: Well, here's John; he'd like to talk to you.

Linda: OK.

John: Hi, Linda!

Linda: Hi. What do you like to do?

John: I like to discover new things, invent new ideas, uh . . . go to the beach . . . uh . . . enjoy . . .

Kaufman: The show's host is a self-confessed personal-ad voyeur. She wrote a book on how to play the personals and promoted it on the talk-show circuit.

Susan: And sometimes what I'd do with a call-in show is, somebody would call in, and—say it was Linda—and I would make up a personal for Linda. And she would express herself and then get off the air. And then maybe Bob would call in and say, "Hey, that Linda, she sounded great, how can I meet her?" And I would just feel terrible that I couldn't match up poor Bob and poor Linda, who were two single people who needed each other. And I thought, "I'm gonna do a show like this myself. I'm gonna match people up on the air," and that's how *Date Night* started.

Kaufman: The banter is that of a singles bar. What kind of work do you do? What movies have you seen? And do you like Chinese food?

Female Voice: What are your favorites?

Male Voice: Sizzling chicken, and hot and sour soup, and all kinds of great stuff.

Female Voice: All right . . .

Susan: I'll bet there are some other sizzling things you can think of to do.

Male Voice: Oh, yes, yes . . .

Female Voice: As long as we can pick and choose, and share plates, and . . .

Male Voice: Definitely.

Female Voice: There are a lot of other things too.

Male Voice: But you gotta use chopsticks.

Female Voice: Oh, I do all the time!

Male Voice: Good.

Kaufman: One of the things you do on the show is you have personal ads.

Susan: Yes. These are little messages that people make up. They can be anywhere from fifteen seconds to a minute long, and they're like the personals in the paper, except they're audio version. And . . . uh . . . you not only get information about people, you get a sense of their personality through their voice, and the best ones have music in the background to enhance the personality. Now, here's Robert, number 603.

Robert: Hi. I'm Robert, and I'm forty-three years old, six feet tall, 165 pounds, and I'm in excellent L.A. condition. I'm a passionate eccentric, and I am definitely an acquired taste. Some women have found me very beautiful.

Susan: I don't like the bland ads that I see in the paper. I don't like when everybody sounds like another single white female . . . uh . . . you know, professional, attractive, articulate, walks on the beach, sensuous, you know, blah, blah, blah, and so on and so forth, you know what I mean? I mean, it's all the same. Now, when people call in to put ads on my show, I tell them, "Look, I want you to be yourself, I mean, the part of you that is different." I don't care how bland a person they may seem to be on the outside, they'll sound outrageous on a personal.

Female Voice: I'm thirty-seven, and I look OK. I don't believe I've ever embarrassed anybody I went out with. I'm lookin' for somebody who's . . . uh . . . lookin' for somebody, I guess. I guess that says it: just a-lookin' for somebody that's lookin' for somebody. And my name's Annie. That's all.

Susan: That is as personal as we can get tonight, folks. This is Susan Block's *Date Night*. Tune in next week; same time, same station, for another Saturday night on *Date Night*.

UNIT 11:
THERE ARE WORSE THINGS THAN DYING

Jason Gaes: My name is Jason Gaes. I live at 1109 Omaha Avenue in Worthington, Minnesota. I am eight years old and I have cancer.

Renee Montaigne: Jason is now nine years old. He's written a book. It's been printed in his own handwriting, titled *My book for kids with cansur*. Adults provided the subtitle, *A Child's Autobiography of Hope*. In the book, Jason describes how he was treated for cancer diagnosed when he was six years old with a rare and fast-spreading form of cancer called Burkitt's lymphoma.

Jason: Radiation is really easy. All you have to do is lay there, and they put straps around your head so you don't move. And then it's over, and you come back tomorrow. But don't wash the Xs off of your head until they're done.

Montaigne: Jason, that's page three of the book, and there's a picture here, of, I guess it's you . . .

Jason: Yeah.

Montaigne: . . . lying on a table . . .

Jason: Mm-hm.

Montaigne: . . . and the word *radiation*. Who drew the picture?

Jason: My two brothers, Adam and Tim. They're better than me, so I let them draw the pictures.

Montaigne: But you wrote the whole book.

Jason: Yeah.

Montaigne: There are books out for kids with cancer. You must have seen them when you first found out you had cancer?

Jason: One time I came home with a . . . a book, and it was called *Hang Tough*, and I thought it was really neat because that boy was going through the same . . . same things as I was going through, and the last two or three pages it told about . . . he died, and . . . and it stunk.

Montaigne: It stunk?

Jason: Uh-huh.

Montaigne: 'Cause he died?

Jason: Uh-huh. I didn't plan for that boy to die because he wrote such a nice book and all. When I wrote this book, I . . . uh . . . I kinda insteada tellin' about Jason Gaes died . . . uh . . . said that Jason Gaes lived.

Montaigne: In one page you write that having cancer isn't fun.

Jason: It ain't no party.

Montaigne: But you . . . you point out a couple of fun things.

Jason: Uh . . . I get lotsa nice presents, 'n' your mom almost does anything you want her to do.

Montaigne: You also write about the different things that a kid would have to go through.

Jason: Mm-hm.

Montaigne: What were the parts that weren't so easy?

Jason: The bone marrow and the spinals and the leg pains are probably the worst of it all. I had to have lots of help for the . . . for the bone marrow because . . . I was almost purple, 'cause it hurt so much.

Montaigne: And the spinal tap. You have a picture here of a little boy, curled up tight.

Jason: Mm-hm. If you do that, it goes a lot faster.

Montaigne: Mrs. Gaes, Jason, in his book, writes about some bad moments.

Mrs. Gaes: Mm-hm.

Montaigne: How did he hold up?

Mrs. Gaes: For the most part, very, very well. Jason . . . uh . . . insisted on not being treated as a sick child. There were times when he needed me and I needed him, when, you know, like right in the middle of a spinal. But otherwise he came right out of the room and . . . went back to his normal activities.

Montaigne: Jason, you wrote this book because you said you were tired of reading books about kids who had cancer and who died in the end. Was there any time during all this treatment when you thought maybe dying wouldn't be so bad?

Jason: When it was all over with, 'cause I thought I like, I would die if, um, right in the middle of a bone marrow.

Mrs. Gaes: About six months into treatment, Jason had had a lot of very aggressive treatment that left him very weak and very sick. And sometimes on the way up to Rochester, we'd stop on the interstate and Jason would become so apprehensive that he would start to vomit before we got there. And I stopped, on the interstate, to help him—he was sick to his stomach—and he just looked at me and said, "Mom, I don't want to do this anymore." And I told him, "Well, you . . . you know what will happen, Jason, if we don't do this." And he told me, "Yeah, but there are worse things than dyin'." And when I read his book, I was stunned, because I . . . I guess I didn't realize how well he had dealt with the possibility of death and dying. If you read his book, you'll see that he compares death to coming out of my womb. He says "When I was a baby in my mom's stomach, I didn't want to come out. The doctor had to give my mom a shot to make me come out. But now that I'm outside, I would never want to go back in my mom's stomach." And he said, "I think going to heaven is like that. Once we get there, we won't want to come back here." So he had no paralyzing fear of dying. It was the treatment, the pain that they would inflict upon him that he was afraid of.

Jason: If you get scared and can't quit, go and talk to your mom, and she can rock you or rub your hair. Or if you want, you can call me. My number is 507-376-3824. And when you feel real bad, it's OK to cry.

Montaigne: Jason, have kids called you?

Jason: Yeah, you bet! Lots of kids have called me. One little girl was gonna have . . . well, she's about my age, she'd be seven right now, and she asked me, um, what she should do 'cause she was gonna have a treatment the day after she called me, and I kinda told her that you can't feel anything after the . . . thing is done. You'll feel a little dry, and sick to your stomach, but to me there was really nothin' wrong with the operation.

Montaigne: Has anyone called you back to tell you

that it helped to talk to you before they had something done?

Jason: Yeah, this, matter of fact, the same little girl. She said that it really worked.

Montaigne: Jason Gaes, along with his mother Sissy. Jason is the author of *My book for kids with cansur.* Doctors have now told Jason that his cancer is completely cured and that there's no chance for a relapse.

Jason: And the rest of the days, when you don't have treatments, try to forget you have cancer and think about something else. Shoot baskets, or go swimming.

UNIT 12
A HEALTHIER WAY OF LOOKING AT MEN AND WOMEN

Katie Davis: This week, Defense Secretary Les Aspin ordered the United States military to end its restrictions on women flying combat missions and serving aboard warships. The move was greeted with applause from many, including Mary Frances Berry, a former member of the U.S. Civil Rights Commission. Berry believes the new policy will alter the way men and women perceive each other and themselves.

Mary Frances Berry: We will begin to think about women and women will think of themselves not only as being shot or being bombed, but women who are able to be defenders of the nation and who are able to wield arms themselves as men do. And that caretakers, therefore—one does not have to assume that caretakers have to be either timid people who have to be protected or that they must be somehow female. It may tear down the boundaries which very much need to be abandoned. And so I think that looking at women in a different way and seeing that men and women may shoot—[*laugh*] that they can be shooters as well as the persons who are being shot—will help us to enlarge our notions about these roles.

Davis: But in a way, it's disturbing to think of women as people who can kill people. It could have some sort of negative repercussions.

Berry: The only way it can have negative repercussions is if we think that it's all right to think of men as people who kill people but not to think of women as people who kill people. What we really ought to think about is that people can kill people if they need to do it for defensive purposes or in wartime or in military occupations. And no one should kill other people.

This is not—no one enjoys war, and the idea is not to contemplate the notion of relishing a military activity. But the idea—men should not relish either. No one should relish it because war is a very unpleasant business. Someone said "War is hell." Sherman, I think, said that—General Sherman. And it is. But the idea is that if in this hellish business that takes place, that everyone who is a citizen in our society is responsible for sharing the burden.

Davis: Does that—

Berry: And that's healthy. That is healthy. It's a healthier way of looking at men, and it's a healthier way of looking at women. And it's a healthier way of raising children. For example, there's no reason why G.I. Joe or this toy that they have, G.I. Joe, shouldn't be G.I. Jane, and they can both either have guns or they both can be fem . . . pacifists or be whatever they are. And so we shouldn't just see men as the people who are military types and they are the ones with the guns.

Davis: Not only will American society have to think about women differently, and, as you said, they will have to think about men differently. And I'm just wondering if we could go into that a little bit more?

Berry: Yes please do. Yeah.

Davis: How so? What—how will men have to view themselves differently?

Berry: Men will have to view themselves not as people who are supposed to protect women all the time but as people who can be protected themselves. For example, a woman might protect them. I could see a military situation where a woman in combat has to be the shooter or the bomber or whatever it is, a bombardier, who is saving the lives of large numbers of men. And when we think about—and so the men will have to see themselves as being people who can be vulnerable and can be protected in the same way that women can.

Davis: Do you think that will really happen? It just seems optimistic to me to think that men would actually accept the role of being vulnerable, being frightened, and that a woman might go out and actually protect him from an enemy attack.

Berry: Well, the minute we have—we have had military situations where women have behaved in a protective fashion by accident or because they happen to have been there. I mean, that has happened. With this policy, the minute we have military enterprise, when on a large scale, lots of women are in combat situations and men find themselves sharing the offense or the defense of being protected by women, everybody is going to say, "Great. Hey, we thought it was going to be a problem. It's not a problem." And that's what will happen.

But I don't want to give the impression that people's minds will be changed automatically and overnight. We are so socialized to believe in these traditional categories of what is male and what is female and that combat is not included. A lot of people will have a hard time accepting that. A lot of people in the military will have a hard time adjusting to that. Some women may have, in their own heads, a hard time adjusting to it. But over time, just as we were socialized to think one way, we can be socialized to believe another way.

And because there's no practical reason to have this policy; it doesn't make any sense to have it. Why should men take more risks to have their lives—lose their lives—than women do in a situation? If women are going to be in the military—and they are—and they ought to have that as an option—they ought to take the same risks.

Davis: Mary Frances Berry is a professor of history and law at the University of Pennsylvania. Her new book is *The Politics of Parenthood.*

ANSWER KEY

UNIT 1

If It Smells Like Fish, Forget It

3. VOCABULARY
Exercise 1

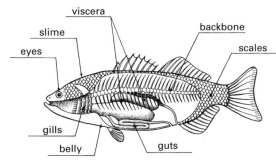

Exercise 2
1. j   2. b   3. i   4. e   5. a   6. h   7. f   8. c
9. d   10. g

4. TASK LISTENING
The eyes

5. LISTENING FOR MAIN IDEAS
Part 1: a   Part 2: a   Part 3: a   Part 4: b   Part 5: c

6. LISTENING FOR DETAILS
Part 1: 1. F   2. T   3. T   4. T   5. F   6. F
Part 2: 7. T   8. F   9. T   10. T   11. F   12. T
         13. T
Part 3: 14. T   15. F   16. T   17. T   18. T
Part 4: 19. F   20. F   21. T   22. T   23. T   24. F
Part 5: 25. T   26. F   27. T

7. LOOKING AT LANGUAGE
Exercise 2
1. the sweeter, the more delicious   2. the redder, the
leaner   3. the riper, the better   4. the more pungent,
the more refined   5. the longer, the smoother   6. the
longer, the less fresh

Exercise 3
1. The greener the peel, the less ripe the banana.
2. The redder the tomato, the greater the chance it
   tastes rotten.
3. The better the quality, the higher the cost.
4. The more natural the fruit juice, the less sweet the
   taste.
5. The more beautiful the raspberries, the more
   delicious the taste.
6. The more additives the food has, the longer it lasts.
7. The softer its interior, the riper the avocado.

8. FOLLOW-UP ACTIVITIES
A. Taking Notes to Prepare
Who should inspect the fish:
• the customer
Consideration of blood:
• blood should be on the backbone
• red blood = not old
• blood can be washed away so people can't see if
  it's old
Consideration of the belly shape:
• nice belly shape
• looks like it's reattaching itself
• not flat
• has the shape of one with viscera inside
• holds its shape; doesn't curl in on itself
Consideration of the outside of a fish:
• the more slime, the better
• scaly, not patchy
Consideration of the eyes:
• cloudy eyes not an indication of freshness
• ice clouds eyes
• spoiled fish can have glassy, clear eyes
• eyes not a great indicator
Consideration of the gills:
• farm-raised fish come intact
• you won't see gills in gutted fish
• bloody is better
Requirements of a quality fish supplier:
• no smell when you sniff
• if it smells like fish, their practices are not good
• fresh fish don't smell

UNIT 2

Living through Divorce

3. VOCABULARY
1. b   2. h   3. g   4. i   5. a   6. d   7. f   8. e
9. c   10. j

4. TASK LISTENING
Her parents are getting divorced.

5. LISTENING FOR MAIN IDEAS
Part 1: c   Part 2: b   Part 3: c

6. LISTENING FOR DETAILS
Part 1: 1. F   2. T   3. T   4. T   5. T   6. F   7. F
         8. F   9. F
Part 2: 10. F   11. T   12. T   13. F   14. F   15. F
         16. T   17. T   18. F
Part 3: 19. T   20. T   21. F   22. F   23. F   24. T

7. LOOKING AT LANGUAGE
Exercise 1
The sender's address
The date
The salutation
The body
Special greeting
The close
The signature

Exercise 2

FORMAL EXPRESSIONS	INFORMAL EXPRESSIONS
Dear Mr. McCarthy:	Dear Eric,
Dear Sir:	Take care.
To whom it may concern:	Write soon.
All the best.	Love,
I look forward to hearing from you.	Fondly,
Sincerely,	
Yours truly,	

8. FOLLOW-UP ACTIVITIES
A. Taking Notes to Prepare
Advice given to Betsy:
- it's important to share feelings
- remember that you are loved and that people care about you
- a lot of kids have the same problem (300/400)
- most people have divorced parents and get through it
- read another book

Persons giving advice to Betsy:
- the mayor of New York (Mayor Koch)
- her guidance counselor
- the interviewer (Noah Adams)
- a psychologist (the author of *The Boys' and Girls' Book of Divorce*)
- her mom

Betsy's questions and feelings about divorce:
- who should she turn to?
- how to get used to her dad being with someone else
- hurt that her parents don't sit together at her dance recital
- why did her parents get divorced?
- what happened to her parents?
- why did her father pack up and leave?

Betsy's advice to others:
- it's not your fault
- it's OK to be sad and cry
- tell someone about your feelings

UNIT 3
A Couch Potato

3. VOCABULARY
1. print money   2. oatmeal   3. secretary
4. abandon   5. workplace   6. pride   7. disease
8. ice 9. telephone 10. chemistry   11. quality

4. TASK LISTENING
The holidays

5. LISTENING FOR MAIN IDEAS
Part 1: a   Part 2: c   Part 3: c   Part 4: c

6. LISTENING FOR DETAILS
Part 1: 1. T   2. F   3. F   4. F   5. T
Part 2: 6. F   7. T   8. F
Part 3: 9. F   10. T   11. F   12. T   13. T   14. F
Part 4: 15. T   16. T

7. LOOKING AT LANGUAGE
Exercise 2
1. Type B, b
2. Type B, a
3. Type A, b
4. Type B, b
5. Type B, c
6. Type B, a
7. Type A, c
8. Type B, b
9. Type B, a
10. Type A, b

8. FOLLOW-UP ACTIVITIES
A. Taking Notes to Prepare
Robert Armstrong's arguments in favor of couch potatoes:
- gets the family together
- people suffer from intellectual guilt
- gives you the needed ballast to stay on the couch
- "If it's on TV, it must be good."

UNIT 4
The Bible Hospital

3. VOCABULARY
1. b 2. g 3. i 4. k 5. f 6. e 7. j 8. a 9. d
10. c 11. h

4. TASK LISTENING
The cookbook

5. LISTENING FOR MAIN IDEAS
Part 1: b   Part 2: c   Part 3: a   Part 4: c

6. LISTENING FOR DETAILS
Part 1: 1. T   2. T   3. F   4. F   5. F
Part 2: 6. T   7. F   8. T   9. F
Part 3: 10. F   11. T   12. T   13. F   14. T
Part 4: 15. T   16. F   17. T   18. T   19. F   20. T

7. LOOKING AT LANGUAGE
Exercise 2
1. twice or two   2. against   3. reverse; undo
4. stop; refuse   5. put in, on   6. not   7. between
8. bad; wrong   9. before   10. one; the same

Exercise 3
1. b   2. b   3. b   4. a   5. a   6. b   7. b   8. a
9. b   10. a

8. FOLLOW-UP ACTIVITIES
A. Taking Notes to Prepare
What Kirby's business gives people:
  • sentimental value
  • preserves dates
  • preserves notes, checks, tips
The similarities between Kirby's business today and his father's business in 1939:
  • the stamper
  • the cutter
  • the little vise backer
The future of Kirby's business:
  • children aren't interested
  • doesn't know what will happen when he's gone
  • maybe just sell the business someday and retire

UNIT 5

A Boy's Shelter for Street People

3. VOCABULARY
1. wealthy people   2. calming   3. relented
4. wise   5. salary   6. charge   7. comprehension
8. politically   9. caring   10. religion

4. TASK LISTENING
His father, Frank Ferrell

5. LISTENING FOR MAIN IDEAS
Part 1: c   Part 2: b   Part 3: a   Part 4: b

6. LISTENING FOR DETAILS
Part 1: 1. a   2. c   3. a   4. a   5. b
Part 2: 6. c   7. c   8. b   9. a   10. b   11. c
Part 3: 12. a   13. b   14. a   15. a
Part 4: 16. b   17. a   18. b   19. b

7. LOOKING AT LANGUAGE
Exercise 2
1. Food is donated to the homeless by fast-food chains.
2. Free food is given to the homeless by volunteers.
3. The homeless were helped by Trevor.
4. Trevor was interviewed by a journalist.
5. The shelter was named "Trevor's Place" by the homeless people.

Exercise 3
1. put   2. was interviewed   3. was published
4. sent   5. was donated   6. volunteered
7. contributed   8. started   9. was opened
10. was named

8. FOLLOW-UP ACTIVITIES
A. Taking Notes to Prepare
Street people's reactions to Trevor's kindness:
  • said "God bless you"
  • a lot of different reactions, all good
  • they all accept the food
  • some might not accept the food—they wear them down to accept it
  • grateful
Trevor's feelings about the people living on the street:
  • he wanted to do something for them right away
  • close friends with many of them
  • people may look scary, but they're really nice
  • we shouldn't treat people by the way they look
  • scared at first but now knows there's nothing to be afraid of
Reasons why people live on the street:
  • some lost their jobs
  • mental problems
  • drink

UNIT 6

The Four New Food Groups

3. VOCABULARY
1. e   2. h   3. j   4. i   5. g   6. c   7. b   8. d
9. f   10. a

4. TASK LISTENING
Possible answers: dairy, meat

5. LISTENING FOR MAIN IDEAS
Part 1: c   Part 2: b   Part 3: b   Part 4: c
Part 5: c

6. LISTENING FOR DETAILS
Part 1: 1. c   2. b   3. a
Part 2: 4. c   5. a   6. c
Part 3: 7. b   8. b
Part 4: 9. b   10. b   11. c   12. a   13. a
Part 5: 14. a

7. LOOKING AT LANGUAGE
Exercise 2
1. eat, will grow up   2. center, will live
3. eat, consume   4. consume, will build
5. is consumed, leeches   6. eat, maintain
7. are, are   8. change, will have   9. eat, risk

8. FOLLOW-UP ACTIVITIES
A. Taking Notes to Prepare
Current four food groups:
   • meat
   • fruits and vegetables
   • dairy products
   • bread and cereal
Proposed four food groups:
   • grains
   • legumes
   • vegetables
   • fruits
Beliefs about current four food groups:
   • dairy products lead to strong bones
Problems with current four food groups:
   dairy:
      • doesn't work to keep strong bones or
        prevent osteoporosis
      • high fat content
   meat:
      • protein leeches calcium out of bones
      • never really low-fat
      • heart attacks
      • people are fatter than they want to be
      • breast cancer
Advantages of proposed four food groups:
   • no cholesterol
   • high in fiber
   • people will live longer
   • people will have healthier lives

UNIT 7
The Dirty Dozen

3. VOCABULARY
1. rocks   2. scatter   3. natural fiber   4. rare
5. threat   6. push up   7. give up   8. throw up
9. compost   10. awards

4. TASK LISTENING
Possible answers: Styrofoam cups, plastic eating
utensils, plastic beverage bottles

5. LISTENING FOR MAIN IDEAS
Part 1: b   Part 2: c   Part 3: a   Part 4: a
Part 5: b

6. LISTENING FOR DETAILS
Part 1: 1. T   2. F   3. F   4. T
Part 2: 5. F   6. T   7. F   8. F
Part 3: 9. T   10. T   11. F   12. T   13. F   14. F
Part 4: 15. T   16. T   17. F
Part 5: 18. T   19. F   20. F   21. T   22. F

7. LOOKING AT LANGUAGE
Exercise 2
   1. I'd like to know if/whether volunteers found
      garbage on the beaches.
   2. Do you remember if/whether the garbage was
      mostly composed of plastic?
   3. Can you tell me if/whether medical waste is the
      biggest problem on beaches?
   4. Please tell me if/whether Styrofoam is one of the
      dirty-dozen items that litter the beach.
   5. Do you know if/whether the things we find on
      beaches are recyclable?
   6. I want to ask if/whether marine life gets hurt by
      plastic.
   7. Tell me if/whether fish stop eating and starve when
      they get entangled.
   8. Do you know/whether any northern fur seals died
      this year?
   9. I'd like to find out if/whether cruise ships are the
      only boats responsible for the dumping.
  10. I wonder if/whether beach communities will have
      to spend much money to clean up beaches.

8. FOLLOW-UP ACTIVITIES

A. Taking Notes to Prepare

Types of garbage found on beaches:
- cigarette butts
- trash
- medical waste
- Styrofoam cups
- plastic eating utensils
- plastic beverage bottles
- metal cans
- glass bottles

Problems that garbage can cause:
- threatens marine life
    - tangled up
    - eat it and feel full
    - starve
- costs millions of dollars to clean up beaches

Attempts to deal with the garbage problem:
- volunteers comb beaches to pick up trash
- Marpol Annex Five treaty (no dumping of plastics)
- Coast Guard investigates
- Coast Guard enforces fines

UNIT 8

From One World to Another

3. VOCABULARY

1. poll 2. ignore 3. study 4. produce 5. house
6. separate from 7. joined 8. glance at 9. neglect
10. creation

4. TASK LISTENING

She is a native American Indian (Oneida and Mohawk).

5. LISTENING FOR MAIN IDEAS

Part 1: b Part 2: a Part 3: c Part 4: a

6. LISTENING FOR DETAILS

Part 1: 1. a 2. b 3. a 4. b
Part 2: 5. a 6. c 7. c
Part 3: 8. c 9. c 10. c
Part 4: 11. a 12. a 13. b

7. LOOKING AT LANGUAGE

Exercise 1

1. high 2. Smoke 3. promise 4. air 5. brush
6. west 7. melting 8. know 9. snow 10. miles
11. morning 12. feather 13. broken 14. dark
15. air 16. dreams

Exercise 2

ANIMALS AND PARTS OF THE BODY OF AN ANIMAL	PLANTS	TIME OF DAY	WEATHER	DESCRIPTIVE VERBS
horses	cedar	moon	breeze	trembling
tails	grasses	darkness	snow	glow
crickets		morning		lumbers
ice bear				gleams
feather				melting
gull				brush
down				breathe
				dying

8. FOLLOW-UP ACTIVITIES

A. Taking Notes to Prepare

Feelings about life on the reservation (Oneida):
- everything is connected
    - the people
    - the land
    - the long-ago
- sense of community

Feelings about life off the reservation (Green Bay):
- exiled
- large place she didn't understand
- didn't feel connected to the other people around her

Reasons why she became a poet:
- poetry made her feel connected to things
- her grandmother's voice
    - told stories
    - loved poetry
- in language she found pictures in her mind
- her father tried to get her to listen and pay attention

UNIT 9

Attached to Crime

3. VOCABULARY

1. violence 2. similar 3. distracted 4. agreement
5. fighter 6. concentrate on 7. delightful 8. tiny
9. feel praised 10. advertised 11. calmer
12. supportive

4. TASK LISTENING

c. the students

5. LISTENING FOR MAIN IDEAS

Part 1: a Part 2: b Part 3: c Part 4: a
Part 5: a Part 6: a

6. LISTENING FOR DETAILS
Part 1: 1. b   2. b
Part 2: 3. b   4. b   5. a   6. b   7. c   8. c
Part 3: 9. c   10. c   11. b
Part 4: 12. a   13. c
Part 5: 14. a   15. b   16. c   17. b   18. c
Part 6: 19. b   20. b

7. LOOKING AT LANGUAGE
Exercise 1
"Crisis of violence, a menace to childhood"
"Violence hits one in four students"
"Our children are growing up scared"

Exercise 2
1. One Wakefield student explained that it did affect her because she had a little brother, and she was scared that he was going to go on drugs.
2. Another student added that in his neighborhood it was becoming like that.
3. A third student admitted that his family knew two people that had had sons or daughters murdered.
4. Another student reported that there had been somebody raped right at the corner of his street.
5. Heather suggested that now that they'd grown up with it . . . they had gotten attached to it.
6. Kassen declared that he knew that he was going to die some way, somehow, so he didn't worry about it.
7. Koon said that she just didn't think that crimes or whatever would come to her because she just didn't feel like it was going to happen to her.

8. FOLLOW-UP ACTIVITIES
A. Taking Notes to Prepare
Examples of crime:
- weapons taken to school
- drugs
- shootings
- murders
- drive-bys
- rapes
- robberies
- weapons at parties

Teenagers' feelings about crime:
- calm acceptance
- the norm
- seek safety in numbers in gangs
- attached to crime
- want to run or move
- don't worry about getting killed
- defiant

Attempts to deal with the crime issue:
- conflict-resolution programs
- beepers and weapons have been banned
- security guards on walkie-talkies

UNIT 10
Meet You on the Air

3. VOCABULARY
1. place   2. married   3. long discussion   4. wife
5. destroy   6. argument   7. cold   8. average
9. outrageous

4. TASK LISTENING
Playing the piano, going to the beach, eating Chinese food

5. LISTENING FOR MAIN IDEAS
Part 1: a   Part 2: b   Part 3: a   Part 4: c

6. LISTENING FOR DETAILS
Part 1: 1. c   2. b   3. c   4. c
Part 2: 5. a   6. a
Part 3: 7. a   8. c   9. c
Part 4: 10. c   11. c   12. b   13. a   14. a   15. b

7. LOOKING AT LANGUAGE
Exercise 1
1. c   2. d   3. f   4. b   5. e   6. a

Exercise 2
1. Some people don't want to give it up just to have a steady boyfriend or girlfriend.
2. It is common for a man to pick her up at her place.
3. People who are engaged to be married sometimes call it off just before the wedding.
4. Some women would like to ask men out for a date, but it's hard for them to pick up the phone and call them up.
5. But it's better to check him out before going on the first date.

8. FOLLOW-UP ACTIVITIES
A. Taking Notes to Prepare
Characteristics of persons looking for a date:
- social
- musical
- likes to discover new things
- likes to invent new ideas
- likes to go to the beach
- likes Chinese food
- likes to pick, choose, and share
- uses chopsticks
- forty-three years old
- six feet tall
- 165 pounds
- in excellent condition
- passionate eccentric
- an acquired taste
- very beautiful

- thirty-seven
- looks OK
- never embarrassed anyone she went out with
- lookin' for somebody that's lookin' for somebody

- when you don't have treatments, try to forget you have cancer
  - think about something else
  - shoot baskets
  - go swimming

UNIT 11

There Are Worse Things Than Dying

3. VOCABULARY
1. f 2. a 3. i 4. e 5. j 6. k 7. c 8. d 9. g
10. h 11. b

4. TASK LISTENING
Yes

5. LISTENING FOR MAIN IDEAS
Part 1: c   Part 2: b   Part 3: b   Part 4: c

6. LISTENING FOR DETAILS
Part 1: 1. c 2. c 3. c
Part 2: 4. b 5. b 6. b 7. a
Part 3: 8. c 9. b 10. a
Part 4: 11. b 12. b 13. b

7. LOOKING AT LANGUAGE
1. d 2. g 3. c 4. f 5. a 6. h 7. b 8. e

8. FOLLOW-UP ACTIVITIES
A. Taking Notes to Prepare
Jason's feelings about treatment:
- radiation is really easy
- the bone marrow, spinals, and leg pains were the worst of all
- the bone marrow hurt so much
- afraid of treatment

Jason's feelings about death:
- it stinks when someone dies
- thought he would die in the middle of a bone marrow
- "There are worse things than dying"
- it's like coming out of the womb
- no paralyzing fear of dying

Jason's advice to cancer patients:
- don't wash the Xs off until they're done
- if you get scared and can't quit, go and talk to your mom
- your mom can rock you, or rub your hair
- call Jason at 507-376-3824
- when you feel real bad, it's OK to cry
- you can't feel anything after the thing is done
  a little dry and sick to your stomach
- there's nothing wrong with the operation

UNIT 12

A Healthier Way of Looking at Men and Women

3. VOCABULARY
10, 11, 6, 3, 7, 2, 5, 4, 8, 12, 13, 9, 1

4. TASK LISTENING
Possible answers: Men will become more vulnerable. Women will become protectors.

5. LISTENING FOR MAIN IDEAS
Part 1: c   Part 2: b   Part 3: a   Part 4: b
Part 5: b

6. LISTENING FOR DETAILS
Part 1: 1. a 2. b
Part 2: 3. b 4. c
Part 3: 5. b 6. a 7. a
Part 4: 8. c 9. b
Part 5: 10. c 11. b

7. LOOKING AT LANGUAGE
Exercise 1
1. a 2. b 3. b 4. a 5. b 6. a 7. a 8. b
9. b

Exercise 2
1. have to 2. should 3. are supposed to 4. could
5. ought to 6. may 7. cannot 8. should 9. must
10. will have to

8. FOLLOW-UP ACTIVITIES
A. Taking Notes to Prepare
Reasons women have not (traditionally) served in combat:
- assumed to be caretakers
- assumed to be timid, vulnerable
- men were supposed to protect women

Reasons women (like men) should serve in combat:
- it will alter the way men and women perceive each other and themselves
- women will be defenders of their nation
- tear down the boundaries
- enlarge our notions of male/female roles
  share offense and defense

ACKNOWLEDGMENTS

Many people contributed to the development of this book, both in the ideas for its content and in the refinement of individual activities.

I am especially grateful to my two editors at Addison Wesley Longman, Joanne Dresner and Penny Laporte. Joanne's vision and continual support for my work have helped me complete a second project. Penny's insights and direction during the editing process helped me reshape the book to better meet our objectives. It has been a wonderful experience working with both of them.

I would also like to thank Allen Ascher and Karen Philippidis at Addison Wesley Longman for their helpful insights and contributions to the editing of this second edition.

This second book could never have been possible without the help of my colleagues at The American Language Program. I would like to thank the chairman, Mary Jerome, who has offered me continual support in my academic pursuits. I would also like to thank Frances Boyd, Karen Brockmann, Sally Fairman, Winnie Falcon, Gail Hammer, Sheri Handel, Jane Kenefick, Polly Merdinger, Barbara Miller, David Mumford, David Quinn, Helene Rubenstein, Shelley Saltzman, Janice Sartori, Linda Schlam, Bill Schweers, Jane Sturtevant, Joanne Warren, and Brian Young. Their willingness to try out the materials with their students and provide comments and suggestions for revisions was invaluable. In addition, I would like to give special thanks to Gail Fingado for being an invaluable resource for the grammar exercises in this book and Dick Faust for contributing pun exercises.

I would also like to thank Carole Rosen and Elly Kellman at the English Language Institute, Hunter College, for their feedback on specific units. And special thanks go to my friend and colleague Peter Thomas, for organizing the piloting of the material at Hunter College.

I am particularly indebted to Sherry Preiss of The Language Training Institute for piloting new material for the second edition of this book. As always, her feedback was extremely valuable in the development of these new units. Sherry was an original contributor to this project, and I continue to appreciate her willingness to provide time and insights to these materials. I would also like to thank Andrea DeWit, Georges Kim, Judy Lin, Joyce Munn, and Nancy Wight for piloting new material in the Community English Program at Teachers College and for providing helpful comments.

Once again, I am indebted to the staff at National Public Radio. They have been most supportive in my completing yet another project. Their willingness to see the project through the various stages of development has shown me that they are true educators, as they believe in extending the use of their programming to classroom settings. I am especially grateful to Carolyn Gershfeld, who was the first person to recognize the value of writing a book for intermediate-level students. Because of her enthusiasm for my work, this second project could be realized. I would also like to thank Joanne Wallace for her willingness to take responsibility for the project halfway through its completion. Theodora Brown was extremely helpful in facilitating some of the more difficult legal processes. I thank her for her support and for her warmth. I would like to thank Kirby Wiggins for helping realize the second edition of this book. I am particularly indebted to Wendy Blair, who has remained a valuable resource to this project. Wendy has been a great influence in the design of this book, both in terms of her ideas for selections and her superb production skills. I thank her for her continued interest and support. Finally, I owe many thanks to the librarians at National Public Radio: Jaclin Gilbert, Beth Howard, Sara Levy, Margot McGann, and Lisa Reginbald. They were very helpful in directing me to the level of materials needed for this book and in providing me with ideas for the content of various units.

And finally, I would like to thank my husband, Eric. Without his continual encouragement and belief in my ability to write, a second book would never have been possible.